A MATTER OF
BLACK AND WHITE

....

The Autobiography of
Ada Lois Sipuel Fisher

A MATTER OF
BLACK AND WHITE

···

The Autobiography of
Ada Lois Sipuel Fisher

BY
Ada Lois Sipuel Fisher

WITH
Danney Goble

FOREWORD BY
Robert Henry

UNIVERSITY OF OKLAHOMA PRESS : NORMAN AND LONDON

Text design by Carl Brune.

Library of Congress Cataloging-in-Publication Data

Fisher, Ada Lois Sipuel, 1924–
A matter of black and white: the autobiography of Ada Lois
Sipuel Fisher / by Ada Lois Sipuel Fisher with Danney Goble ;
foreword by Robert Henry.
   p. cm.
   Includes index.
   ISBN 0-8061-2819-4 (alk. paper)
   1. Fisher, Ada Lois Sipuel, 1924– . 2. Afro-Americans—
Oklahoma—Biography. 3. Civil rights workers—Oklahoma
—Biography. 4. Oklahoma—Race relations. 5. Afro-Americans
—Civil rights—Oklahoma. I. Goble, Danney, 1946– . II. Title.
E185.97.F46A3 1996
976.6'00496073'0092–dc20
[B]
                         95-38775
                             CIP

The paper in this book meets the guidelines for permanence
and durability of the Committee on Production Guidelines for
Book Longevity of the Council on Library Resources, Inc. ∞

1 2 3 4 5 6 7 8 9 10

Dedicated to the memory of my beloved husband,
Warren W. Fisher

CONTENTS

ILLUSTRATIONS

Ada Lois's father, Bishop Travis B. Sipuel   7
Ada Lois's mother, Martha Bell Smith Sipuel   9
Ada Lois with neighborhood child and churchwomen   17
Flossie Thompson's piano students   23
Lincoln High School graduation, 1941   56
The Lincoln School band, ca. 1939   57
Ada Lois's senior class picture, 1941   60
Warren W. Fisher as a young soldier   67
The Sipuel family, ca. 1943   77
Dr. George Lynn Cross, president of the University of Oklahoma, ca. 1946   82
Dr. W. A. J. Bullock, Ada Lois, and Roscoe Dunjee at the time of the first attempt to enroll at the University of Oklahoma   88
Leaving Warren, and Rhode Island, after the Supreme Court's favorable decision   123
Ada Lois with her mother at the Oklahoma City airport, ready to enroll at the University of Oklahoma   124
Back in the Oklahoma courts, Thurgood Marshall confers with Harvard's law school dean, Erwin Griswald.   137
Finally a law student, Ada Lois is ready to enter Monnet Hall—the "Law Barn."   146
Ada Lois celebrating graduation with Warren Fisher   151
Ada Lois officially signing the registry of the Oklahoma bar   158
Langston professor Ada Lois Fisher   165
Ada Lois dressed for a formal evening with Warren Fisher   176
Dedication of Chickasha's Ada Sipuel Avenue   186

*Except where noted, all photographs are
courtesy of Ada Lois Sipuel Fisher.*

FOREWORD

....

ROBERT HENRY

What does a legend look like? Do heroines and heroes show their heroism? Do they look like Greek gods, or perhaps Gilbert Stuart portraits? Are they ordinary people, or are they more like purple cows? Do they know their cosmic task from childhood, or is greatness thrust upon them? Do they prepare diligently from youth, or do they play at school, love gingerbread, and make funny rhymes like everyday kids?

I don't know the answers to these questions or the recipe for heroism. I do, however, know a very few such people. Ada Lois Sipuel Fisher is surely one of them.

In 1941 Oklahoma and the rest of the United States were at war. Oklahoma had contributed sacrificially and valiantly to the last war. But this was even more dangerous, as our enemies were drunk with the false vision of racism. Nazi Germany, under the influence of Adolph Hitler, claimed supremacy of the Aryan race and laid claim to Europe; Italy, under Benito Mussolini, sought to recall the grandeur of former days of Roman hegemony by enslaving Ethiopia; Japan, controlled once again by powerful warlords, sought to convince the "children of the sun" that Japanese superiority demanded control of the inferior races that inhabited the rest of Asia.

But even as Oklahoma prepared to fight this racism-inspired conflict abroad, it was, sadly, blind to the racism that existed within its own borders. For also in 1941 the Oklahoma Legislature made it a misdemeanor to teach in a classroom containing both African Americans and whites, and to further ensure the desired result, it was also a misdemeanor even to be a student in such a mixed-race classroom. Unfortunately, such racism was not an unfamiliar part of Oklahoma's history. A noted history, referring to Oklahoma's unique entrance to the Union as a "dry" state (allowing no liquor to be sold), is entitled *Born Sober.* Sadly, another book could justifiably be written about our founding entitled *Born Racist.*

African Americans first came to Oklahoma in significant numbers as slaves of the Indians who were forced to relocate in Oklahoma in the 1830s. Although some evidence exists that Indians were, as compared to whites, not too bad as slave owners, slavery is slavery, and no amount of kindness can civilize that "peculiar institution."

As Oklahoma began its move for statehood, racism continued. When Oklahoma's proposed constitution was drafted, its leading plank was total segregation of schools and transportation facilities. It was small wonder—the primary duo behind the document were not even thinly veiled racists. Charles Haskell, the drafter who later became Oklahoma's first governor, worked strenuously for what he called "race distinctions" such as segregation and preventing or limiting black suffrage. "Alfalfa Bill" Murray, the president and chief architect of the 1906–07 Constitutional Convention, was, at the time of that convention, remarkably generous in his discourse compared to his later rhetoric. The black citizen "must be taught in the line of his own sphere," Murray intoned. And blacks were quite capable "as porters, bootblacks and barbers, and [in] many lines of agriculture" (Levy, "Before *Brown,*" *Extensions* [Fall 1994], 10). This was one of the most benign statements that Murray would make on the subject.

President Theodore Roosevelt rejected the draft of the constitution with the Jim Crow plank. Though the drafters removed the offending passage, the first bill passed by the legislature, Senate Bill 1, reenacted Jim Crow. It took only twelve days to enact.

The original definition of "white" and "colored" remained in the constitution, in Article 23: "Wherever in this Constitution and laws of this state, the word or words, 'colored' or 'colored race,' 'negro' or 'negro race,' are used, the same shall be construed to mean or apply to all persons of African descent. The term 'white race' shall include all other persons." This vastly oversimplified definition was important because of the Article 13 command to provide "separate schools for white and colored children."

Racial tension reached its zenith in 1921 in Tulsa. After a young black man named Dick Rowland was accused of assaulting a white woman on an elevator, rumors of a probable lynching circulated wildly. Because at least 141 lynchings had already occurred in the state, the rumors were credible. Members of the black community armed themselves and gathered around the courthouse to prevent Rowland's removal. Rioting broke out on a massive scale, and at least seventy African Americans and nine whites were killed The Greenwood area of Tulsa, about two square miles of thriving property owned by African Americans, was left a smoking rubble.

Ada Lois Sipuel Fisher knew about all of this and more. Her parents left Tulsa as a consequence of the riot, one of the worst in American history. They moved to Chickasha, a more bucolic setting, but still a place shadowed by racism. After all, the Ku Klux Klan was the dominant power in Oklahoma in the 1920s; having elected one governor and a host of other state and local officials, the Klan was perhaps more powerful in Oklahoma than in any other state.

Mrs. Fisher brilliantly describes the tenor of the times in this important book. If anything, the pressures of racism—and her own heroism—are understated. The tragedies of those times are mitigated by her own nobility, modesty, and greatness of character. Hers is a story of triumph for both African Americans and whites, indeed for all races.

In these troubled times, perhaps we can imagine the difficulties of an impetuous, self-confessed "smart-mouth" girl being the "guinea pig" in an experiment to open Oklahoma's colleges—and the colleges and later primary and secondary schools of the rest of the nation—to African Americans. The Sipuels, Ada's parents, had moved to Chickasha just in time to witness the last documented lynching of an African American in Oklahoma. They also knew about Lloyd Gaines, a young black man who had received a favorable decision from the United States Supreme Court in 1938 in a case seeking to obtain his admission into Missouri's law school. Gaines vanished; his disappearance remains unexplained. Despite these difficulties, challenges, and the obvious danger involved, Ada Lois became the plaintiff in the famous United States Supreme Court case of *Sipuel v. Board of Regents.*

The true significance of *Sipuel* may never be known. But as Professor Dennis J. Hutchison observed:

> Between 1938 and 1948, the year the Supreme Court decided *Sipuel v. Oklahoma State Regents . . . Gaines* [had] provided [only] window-dressing—and nothing else—as the Court slowly and carefully chipped away at racially discriminatory practices involving juries, elections, transportation, and organized labor. At the same time, the Court consistently upheld wartime racial classifications involving Japanese residents.
>
> When the petition for certiorari in *Sipuel* was filed on September 24, 1947, *Gaines* could no longer be regarded merely as a sport. (68 *Georgetown Law Journal* 1, 6)

Sipuel showed that the struggle was not weakening, but in fact was gaining strength. The *Sipuel* brief provided the first direct challenge to the separate-but-equal doctrine with its bold statement: "there can be no separate equality." Although this issue was not pressed in the oral argument, the handwriting was on the wall. *Sipuel* provided the first *unanimous decision* on these matters, showing that the wall of state-sanctioned racism, like the Berlin Wall in the 1980s, was beginning to crack.

Sipuel was an important milestone on the road to *Brown v. Board of Education,* the landmark decision in 1954 that was the beginning of the end of segregated schools. As Judge J. Harvie Wilkinson observed, *Brown* "may be the most important political, social, and legal event in America's twentieth-century history." *Sipuel* was indeed a cornerstone in the building of this key case. As Professor Harry F. Tepker, Jr., noted:

> [in *Brown*] a unanimous Supreme Court led by Earl Warren accepted the principles first articulated by Marshall in *Sipuel*. Exclusion of blacks on the basis of race automatically created a badge of inferiority. No educational opportunity could be equal if the excluded group suffered such stigma. Desegregation, no phony equalization, was the appropriate demand of the Fourteenth Amendment's equal protection clause. (*Sooner Magazine*, Fall 1992, 11)

But *Sipuel* and Ada Lois herself have added meaning for the State of Oklahoma. This young woman, described by then–University of Oklahoma President George Lynn Cross as "chic, charming and well poised," had courage that will long serve as an example for Oklahomans. In a time where heroines—or as one of my judicial friends says, *sheroes*—are greatly needed, the courage of this precocious woman with a gentle heart and a fighting spirit is truly exemplary.

Ada Lois's courageous stand laid the foundation for others. In 1955, when the mandate of *Brown* became clear and desegregation was to proceed "with all deliberate speed," much of the South initially resisted. In Oklahoma, remembering the courage of Ada Lois Sipuel Fisher, Governor Raymond Gary shocked many of his southern colleagues. In his finest hour, eschewing political caution and bucking ignoble tradition, the plain-speaking governor stated, "I grew up in 'Little Dixie,'" but as "an active Baptist and believer in the scriptures . . . I have never understood how persons can call themselves Christians and believe that God made them superior because they were born with white skin" (Scales and Goble, *Oklahoma Politics*, 298).

Raymond Gary's statements merged into commands. He orchestrated an amendment destroying the constitutional scheme of unfair funding to African American schools; it passed three to one. In a state once ruled by the Klan in the 1920s, a governor from "Little Dixie," following the lead of Ada

Lois Sipuel Fisher, officially began the dismantling of a system that guaranteed inequality for daughters and sons of Oklahoma.

Young Americans will have difficulty understanding a time when whites and blacks were forced to use separate restrooms, where blacks were always forced to "move to the back of the bus," where restaurants wouldn't serve them food, and where hotels wouldn't provide lodging. It's difficult to imagine that almost-cosmopolitan Norman, home of the now-thriving University of Oklahoma, was once a "sundown" town where blacks could not stay when the sun set. It's hard to imagine that this fine community once forced Thurgood Marshall, who later became the Solicitor General of the United States, a circuit judge, and a Supreme Court justice, to lunch on peanuts from a vending machine because no city restaurant would serve him. It is almost beyond belief that black students, when they were admitted to college classrooms, were forced to sit in a chair marked "colored," or learn in an alcove out of sight, or dine behind a chain.

Those chairs and alcoves are destroyed, and those chains that held a great nation apart are now largely shattered. Much remains to be done, but the greatest part, the beginning, has been accomplished by a handful of courageous women and men who believed in the rule of law. This is the story of one such heroine.

PREFACE

....

"Purple Cow"
I never saw a purple cow
I never hope to see one.
But I can tell you anyhow
I'd rather see than be one.

—GELETT BURGESS

Every journey has a beginning. Every saga has a starting point. What circumstances or situations caused or merely permitted a given action? Who we are and what we believe depends on all of our life experiences as well as on our immediate responses and reactions. Where does it all begin?

I did not grow up daydreaming of being a test case. By the simple act of applying for admission to the University of Oklahoma, I became a purple cow, a pioneer, the principal figure in a historic court case, a "who does she think she is?" Young people today may well be puzzled by the sound and fury that resulted from a simple request for equality of treatment—the birthright of every American citizen. I want them to be puzzled, because I hope that they cannot relate to or even begin to understand such attitudes. In fact, I am writing this book less to explain those earlier and darker times than to celebrate their passing.

As I write it, I sense a tendency (entirely natural, I suppose) to examine some of the assumptions and attitudes that have sometimes taken me into certain situations, including some where I had never intended to be. In my growing-up years, my folks said that I was guilty of what the elders called "sassing" and "smart-mouthing." What so many took as smart-mouthing was not smart at all. On the contrary: I just could not help wondering about the things I could not understand. I was full, not of sass, but of questions: by what authority, for what purposes, and instead of what alternatives?

Now that I am much older, I sometimes try to put away childish things, and I often counsel myself to remain silent and let another person speak out. Surely someone else also wonders whether a given rule or practice is fair and well founded. Surely others will speak out. Usually, though, they do not. Still, if the objectives are legitimate and the means are fair, I try to go along, even if it requires personal inconvenience. If the ends are illegitimate and the means are unfair, I return to the habits of my youth. My only question is then: Which alternatives are most defensible and most compatible with my own sense of morality and fairness? Even if no one else dares speak up, I must answer that question. And sometimes I answer it aloud.

Speaking of questions: In the spring of 1988 I attended a legal forum at the University of Oklahoma at which Coleman Young, the former mayor of Detroit, was the principal speaker. As we ate lunch, we talked of many things. During a break in the conversation, I noticed him looking intently at me. Then he asked why I had agreed to become the guinea pig in one of the earliest civil rights struggles in this country. He guessed I must have known that the state would resist with all its resources. Yes, I knew that. Was I fairly aware of possible intimidation, harassment, and even physical harm? Yes, I was certainly aware. Then why?, he repeated.

"Look," I said, "the law was wrong. The whole system was unfair."

"True," he said, "but why *you*?"

I could not find then a perfectly satisfactory answer. I have tried since to find a more complete one, and this book is partially the consequence of that effort. But the full and final answer remains contained entirely in the three words that I returned to Mayor Young: "It was wrong."

ACKNOWLEDGMENTS

In telling this story, I have accumulated many new debts and added to existing ones. Chief in the latter category is the debt I continue to compound with my son, Bruce Travis Fisher. Since I first started thinking about recording my life, Bruce has been a steady source of both inspiration and help. In particular, he has used his academic skills as a trained historian to perform much of the research that undergirds this work. That research includes considerable time spent in the archives and newspaper division of the Oklahoma Historical Society to collect old documents, as well as time spent at our home to revive and refresh old memories. That done, Bruce employed his acquired skills with the computer to record all of these materials and to begin shaping them into a systematic and intelligible whole. That this book exists at all is due to his efforts, efforts that managed to be both technical and personal, both professional and loving.

Two old friends, Jerue Hawkins and James Potts, made contributions along the way so numerous and so diverse that they cannot be recorded, merely gratefully acknowledged. Toward the project's end, it also benefited from the considerable research skills and scholarly enthusiasm of Michael Lovegrove. A graduate student in history at the University of Oklahoma, Michael was especially valuable at turning up obscure information about Chickasha, both during my formative years and during my early legal practice there. Michael performed his work under the direction of Dr. Danney Goble, a professional writer and recognized authority on Oklahoma's history. Dr. Goble worked directly with me in shaping the final form of this narrative, thereby making it both a personal statement and a historical document.

A MATTER OF
BLACK AND WHITE

....

*The Autobiography of
Ada Lois Sipuel Fisher*

GENESIS: MY PARENTS

E very child born carries the legacy of both parents. That legacy includes more than twenty-three pairs of elaborate, chemically complex chromosomes. It also includes the history that shaped the lives of both parents. In my case, that history includes some of the more powerful undercurrents of the experiences of many African Americans during the final generation of slavery and the first generation of emancipation.

My father, Travis B. Sipuel, spent nearly all of his adult life as a minister, business manager, and bishop of the Church of God in Christ (COGIC). Today the Church of God in Christ is the world's largest predominantly black denomination in the so-called Pentecostal movement. My father's history—which is to say, one strain of mine—might as well begin with the story of that church. In many ways, it is a story that reminds me of my own. I suspect that it may explain a bit of it, also.

Pentecost was an annual Jewish feast, so called because it fell on the fiftieth day after Passover. According to the second chapter of Exodus, it was also known as the Feast of Weeks and the Feast of Harvest. Pentecostal Christians take their name from the account given in the Book of Acts, when Christ's heartbroken disciples gathered fifty days after His crucifixion. Their grief was broken by a sudden outpouring of the Holy Spirit that empowered them to continue His divine work on earth. The spirit's arrival was marked with tongues of fire that settled on each of those gathered there and made of them a new community that transcended previously divided languages and nations.

Ever since those biblical times, the expectation of another divine act that would create a New Jerusalem—a true community of all believers—has remained a fixed, albeit distant, Christian hope. John Wesley, the staid English founder of

Methodism, shared it, as did Sojourner Truth, the former slave and underground railroad conductor. Neither, of course, lived to see it.

At this century's beginning, many came to believe that they were seeing it. It began to happen, the believers say, on April 14, 1906, at a former livery stable located at 312 Azusa Street in Los Angeles, California. On that day, in that place, William Joseph Seymour ignited the spark that flamed into the worldwide spread of modern Pentecostalism. Without him, my father's life—and my own—no doubt would have been quite different.

William Seymour was born of former slave parents in 1870 in the Mississippi River community of Centreville, Louisiana. With no formal education at all, he taught himself to read, studied the Scriptures, and set out as an itinerant preacher, taking the Gospel to rural communities across the South as well as to some of the larger cities located along its rim. In time he came to share with others the belief that human history was approaching its end and that Christ would return imminently to establish his kingdom. To make way for it, true Christians should come out of their existing denominations— both black and white—to prepare the way for the purified and racially inclusive church that God was anxious to raise.

Seymour believed that he witnessed the sure sign of the latter day by the outpouring of the Holy Spirit when Lucy Farrow, a white member of the congregation, began to pray aloud in what seemed to be an unfamiliar language. Sensing that the woman possessed a rare depth of spiritual intensity, Seymour called her gift "speaking in tongues."

Lucy Farrow later introduced Seymour to her own minister, who ran a Bible school in Houston. Charles Fox Parham was a white man—in fact, some said that he was an active sympathizer of the Ku Klux Klan—but he could not charitably turn away such an obviously earnest seeker. He agreed that Seymour could listen to the professor's lectures while seated on a chair outside the open window of the classroom. In the event of rain, he could sit inside the building, but outside the classroom's open door. I later had reason to know something of that same experience.

In 1906 Seymour conducted a revival in Los Angeles in an abandoned livery that still reeked of horses. He and his friends rented the building, cleaned and whitewashed it, and held services there. This was the beginning of the modern Pentecostal movement. It also helped define it as something new and different.

After all, these were the days in which European colonialists proudly shouldered the "white man's burden" and set off to rule presumedly lesser but certainly darker-skinned peoples. These also were the days in which white southerners terrorized, lynched, disfranchised, and segregated black southerners, in the name of Jim Crow. They were the days, too, in which many white northerners generally greeted that news with sighs of "Good riddance."

It was not the shouting, weeping, and praying that so moved visitors to the Los Angeles revivals. It was the fact that whites and blacks, men and women, were doing all of these things together. One southern white minister at the scene later noted in his diary that he had been initially offended, then startled, but finally inspired by the fact that, as he put it, "the color line was washed away in the blood."

Charles Harrison Mason was born on September 8, 1866, in Shelby County, near Memphis, Tennessee. Like the place of Seymour's birth, it was right in the heart of the lower Mississippi floodplain. Mason's parents, the former slaves Jerry and Eliza Mason, were tenant farmers active in the Missionary Baptist Church. In 1878 the family moved to Plumersville, Arkansas, where Mason experienced conversion. A yellow fever outbreak in the next year took his father's life and threatened his own. On the first Sunday in September 1880, however, Mason was suddenly cured by what he understood to be divine intervention. Baptized shortly thereafter, he set out to preach revivals throughout the flat cotton country of southern Arkansas and northern Mississippi. With only minimal and sporadic formal education, he began to preach a doctrine similar to that then being developed by William Seymour.

In early 1907 Mason made his way to Los Angeles, where he added to his spiritual blessing by attending the Pentecostal revival. Upon his return to the south, Mason persuaded others of the powers of the new revelation and, with them, organized the Church of God in Christ in September 1907. Elected general overseer of the new denomination, Mason accepted the title of bishop and proceeded to preach and organize new churches. Some of these were black, others were white. In fact, in the early years of this century the Churches of God in Christ included as many predominantly white congregations as black. As the recognized leader of a legally charted body, Mason also ordained other Pentecostal ministers, both white and black. One of them was my father, Travis B. Sipuel.

I know little of the background of my father's family and his own early life. I do not even know what the initial "B." in his name stands for. Like Seymour and Mason, he was born in the Deep South of ex-slave parents, near Columbus, Mississippi, in or near the year 1877. He never knew his own father, who had died or disappeared before my father's birth. For that reason, neither he nor any of his descendants have any idea of how the unusual name Sipuel entered the family. When I was a young girl, I sometimes thought that he must have made it up, but my mother told me otherwise. She had actually met a brother of his, Charlie Sipuel; so no, it was not just his invention.

He was raised by his mother and an abusive stepfather on the same Mississippi plantation where his own people had been held as slaves. When he was thirteen or fourteen, he ran away from home and broke all ties with his family. So complete was the break that he rarely spoke of them and never spoke to his children about his early life. In later life, he had a habit of saying, "I shook their dust off my shoes," when he permanently turned away from people; and I suppose that he shook his whole family's dust off when he left the plantation.

ADA LOIS'S FATHER, BISHOP TRAVIS B. SIPUEL

After leaving Mississippi, my father made his way to Birmingham, Alabama, where he worked as a waterboy in the developing steel mills. He later worked for the railroads that crisscrossed the southern states. Although he had even less formal education than William Seymour or Charles Mason, my father was naturally bright and gifted with the qualities of leadership. In time, he became a foreman who oversaw a crew of a dozen men or so that traveled up and down the rail lines, making repairs along the tracks. About all that I know of his work there is that he lost the little finger of his left hand on the job. All of my life, he had nothing but a little nub there. Eventually, his work took him to the little community of Dermott, on the Arkansas side of the Mississippi River. There he met my mother.

My mother was Martha Bell Smith, the daughter of Lucinda Smith. Grandma Cindy, a fair-skinned slave, was the daughter of a slave by that slave's master. As a teenager, she was purchased from a white family in Memphis, Tennessee.

Her purchaser—a man known to my family as "Cap'n Anderson"—turned out to be my grandfather.

Cap'n Anderson carried Grandma Cindy to his plantation near Belarie, Arkansas, in Chicot County. There he raised two separate families "in the same yard." One family was by his wife, a white woman who bore him seven children, the other by my grandmother, who also bore seven. The two sets of children, each child born within two months of its counterpart, were delivered by the same black midwife. One set lived in a large white house in the middle of the plantation. The other, the group that included my mother, lived about a mile away in a small but tidy cabin.

The children of both families played together. In fact, I have heard my mother often speak of her white "brothers" and "sisters." According to family legend, one of the white brothers became a prominent Arkansas politician, who went on to serve the state's (all-white) voters for several years in the capitol at Little Rock. My mother told me that she once had called him when she passed through Little Rock. According to her, his voice joyfully greeted her on the telephone. In fact, he invited her to come by the capitol for a friendly brother-sister visit; but, he added, she would have to keep her "little pickaninnies" away. Mother slammed down the phone. As far as I know, she never spoke to her brother again. His white wife sent her the newspaper clipping that announced the esteemed gentleman's death.

Grandma Cindy's seven children all kept the name Smith, perhaps in ironic tribute to an earlier master. The oldest was Frank, who was born a slave on his own father's plantation in 1862, during the Civil War. The others were Kitty, Lucinda, Nan, Scott, and Gertrude. My mother, Martha Bell Smith, was the youngest, born in 1892.

My mother's memory was that Cap'n Anderson's black children had little use for their white father. When he would call on my grandmother, he often brought them little gifts of candy and the like, but the children all feared him. It was not that he ever beat or otherwise abused them. Instead, it

ADA LOIS'S MOTHER,
MARTHA BELL SMITH SIPUEL

seemed that they all instinctively distrusted the man and rejected what they took to be his immoral ways with their own mother. That attitude always troubled Grandma Cindy, who overlooked the circumstances of their relationship to proclaim that Cap'n Anderson was the only man that she had ever loved and the only man who ever had touched her.

When Frank was a very young man, he built a modest house and moved his mother and younger siblings off the plantation. Mother grew up in Dermott, Arkansas. The family baby, she had the best of what little was available, and she was the only one to receive any substantial education. After finishing Dermott's public schools, she graduated from the little two-year teachers' academy in the town and became a schoolteacher herself.

Stunningly beautiful, with light skin, hazel eyes, and hair that bore the slightest curl, she was teaching when she met my father, a handsome, very dark-skinned railroad man nearly fifteen years older than she. He was smitten hard and immediately. All of Grandma Cindy's fair-skinned children married extremely dark spouses. His greatest drawback seemed to be his age. I remember her telling me that when he came courting she would tell her mother, "Mama, here comes your beau. He must be coming for you; he's too old for me."

Of course, it was the daughter that he sought, and it was the daughter that he won. As soon as they were married, in 1908, my mother taught him to read, using a little Webster's reader that I still have. Not long afterward, a revival came to Dermott. My father and mother were converted to Christ and baptized by the evangelist whose words had transformed their lives. That preacher was Charles Harrison Mason.

Under Bishop Mason's guidance, my father studied the Scriptures and was ordained by the Church of God in Christ as a minister. Soon he began to preach in little churches all across southern Arkansas, sometimes dipping down as far south as Louisiana. He also taught himself bookkeeping, becoming something of a master of the intricate ins and outs of financing struggling Pentecostal congregations. In time, my mother bore him a son, Samuel, but the child died in infancy.

Daddy and Mother moved from Dermott to Tulsa, Oklahoma, in 1918. Dad had earlier attended a religious meeting there and liked the city. He was impressed by the well-kept residential area and the bustling black business community. He rented a house and furnished it comfortably. Daddy leased a building and, with a handful of followers, organized the North Greenwood Church of God in Christ. They passed out handbills and made house-to-house visits, inviting persons to attend and, they hoped, join the new church. The membership slowly grew to about forty.

Tulsa was a good place to be at the time. Recent oil discoveries at nearby places like Red Fork and Glenpool already had attracted men like J. Paul Getty and William G. Skelly to the place that, even then, liked to think of itself as the "Oil Capital of the World." Less prominent persons came, too, by the tens of thousands. Many, like my own family, were African Americans, drawn from Oklahoma's hinterland as well as rural Arkansas and Missouri. Many found jobs in the oil fields. Some found themselves members of the three Church of God in Christ congregations that sprang up on the gray soil of north Tulsa. Most lived in the community along Greenwood Street, north of Archer.

By the time my parents reached Tulsa, Greenwood was known as the "Negro Wall Street." Retail shops, hotels, movie theaters, dozens of clubs, and numerous churches lined its sidewalks or radiated out into the thriving all-black community that surrounded it. It was Jim Crow municipal ordinances and racist real estate practices that kept Greenwood all black, but not even those things could keep it down—or keep it quiet. Particularly on the weekends and Wednesdays (the maids' night out), Greenwood rocked with a mighty chorus of laughter, greetings, curses, and insults. They came from a thousand black throats that had found in the booming oil town on the Arkansas River freedom and opportunities still unknown to little backwater places like Dermott.

I recall my parents' recollection of those times, but I recall much more vividly their account of how they ended. On the last day of May 1921, a young African American named Dick Rowland was accused of assaulting Sarah Page, a white woman, in a downtown Tulsa elevator. The police arrested Rowland and placed him in the county jail. Inspired by racist editorials in the afternoon's *Tulsa Tribune*, two groups gathered that evening on the courthouse green. One was a black group, there to prevent a probable lynching. The other was a white group, uneasy in the presence of so many determined (and armed) blacks. Shouts were exchanged. Then came shots. For the next day or so, Tulsa exploded into one of the nation's earliest and bloodiest race wars. When it was over, Greenwood Avenue lay in smoking ruins. Spread out alongside it were thirty-six square blocks of total destruction. Virtually all of the "Negro Wall Street" and of Tulsa's black-owned property was destroyed.

James B. A. Robertson, the governor of Oklahoma, had dispatched the state militia to preserve order, but Tulsa's

blacks knew that the only real effect had been to give the riot-
ers a free hand by seizing and holding their community's
black defenders. One of those was my father, whom the militi-
amen spirited away to a holding pen in Tulsa's McNulty Park.
With the community defenseless, the rioting continued until
there was nothing left to burn. Included in the destruction
was the little house that my mother and father had bought
and furnished. A militia officer had noticed my mother standing across the street, watching her own home go up in
flames.

"Lady, what are you doing here?" he asked.

My mother could not even choke out a response.

"Well," the white captain told her, "you'd better get your-
self back to the white part of town before the niggers get
ahold of you."

Shortly thereafter, both my mother and my father got
themselves out of Tulsa and made their way to Chickasha,
Oklahoma, where they settled in the "colored" part of town.

GROWING UP IN GRADY'S NEW SOUTH

C hickasha, where my parents relocated after the Tulsa disaster, was the county seat and the only town of any size in Grady County, which had been formed when Oklahoma entered the union in 1907. The county's population was largely of southern extraction, hailing from Texas and Arkansas. Like other counties in the southwestern part of the state, it honored a prominent southerner with its name. In this case, the honoree was Henry W. Grady, the publisher and editor of the *Atlanta Constitution* and a tireless propagandist for a so-called New South. Its newness supposedly derived from an urban and industrial civilization that would replace the tired plantation economy and rural society of the Old South. Not least of its new features was to be a mature and permanent resolution of the region's ages-old "race question." In Mr. Grady's New South, the two races would be separated by a firm but civil wall of segregation. It would begin at birth in segregated hospitals, continue through schooling in segregated schools, and end with burial in segregated cemeteries. That was, so the majority's thinking went, the only way in which the two races could peaceably and profitably coexist.

Except in the last regard, neither Grady County nor the community of Chickasha turned out to be very different from the Old South after all. The countryside sprouted green cotton plants every spring, their stalks kept clear of weeds by hoes wielded by black hands. In the fall, black hands stripped the fluffy fields of their white cotton bolls.

Cotton was one of several staple crops. It had to share its regal throne with the watermelons grown in Rush Springs and the broom corn produced at nearby Lindsay, communities that claimed the respective titles of "Watermelon Capital" and "Broom Corn Capital" of the world. Neither probably faced serious international jealousy over its self-assigned title. Probably more important than any of these crops was the livestock that fed on the county's lush grasses that carpeted the valley of the Washita River and lay on the undulating plains aside the river's many tributary creeks.

As for urban and industrial splendor, Chickasha's population (10,179 in 1920, on its way to 14,099 in 1930) made it Oklahoma's tenth largest city in the latter year. Nonetheless, the only real industry was found in the rail yards of the Rock Island, which served the area's farming population. The oil boom that was awakening much of Oklahoma barely echoed in the county, and drilling and refining were unheard of in the city.

The area had always had a substantial African American population. The Chickasaw Indians, whose nation had included the county, had brought their slaves with them during their own relocation from the Old South back in the early 1800s. Many black families who lived there a century later could trace their ancestry to those people and their freed descendants. In that regard, many African Americans had lived there much longer than the whites, most of whom came to the area only after about 1899. After the abolition of slavery, black emigrants came of their own free will, and they carried the hopes of free people with them. Their migration was proof that they did not accept the tenets of the Old South. By 1930 these numbered 1,625 in Chickasha, five of whom were the Sipuels.

I am not sure why my parents chose Chickasha as the target of their exodus, but my guess is that it must have involved my father's work. Chickasha's black population already supported seven or eight small churches, but nearly all of them were aligned with the Baptist or Methodist denominations. Until my father came on the scene, there was no Church of God in Christ there, and my father likely saw the opportunity to build one. In the nature of things, his new church would have to be all or nearly all black, since the early interracial Pentecostal movement had already split upon the rock of American racism with the breakaway of white believers to form the Assemblies of God in 1914. That itself was something of a symbol of what the New South would be, and it meant that my father would labor in its darker vineyards.

His was a rich and full harvest. He rented a small house for his wife and the children he hoped to have. He then went to work building a congregation and a church. In a few years, the congregation numbered forty or fifty. Soon my parents owned their own home next door to the church, on East Dakota Avenue.

After her first-born, Samuel, had died back in Arkansas, Mother despaired of ever being able to produce more children. In time, she took her grief to Bishop Mason at a church conference and asked him to pray that she might be able to conceive and bear a child. He did so—in fact, the bishop laid his hand on her head, anointed her with oil, and promised to keep her in his prayers. After a few months (not much more than nine), she bore a son, Lemuel. At the next conference, she delighted Bishop Mason with the news. He blessed her, reanointed her, and promised to continue his prayers. In short order, I was born—the date was February 8, 1924—and the good bishop continued to pray. By the next church conference, my mother had delivered yet another child, Helen Marie. This time mother approached Bishop Mason with a revised plea. "Pap" (she always called him "Pap" Mason), "you can stop praying—I now have enough." Mother had no more children.

The three of us—known most of our lives as Big Sip (Lemuel), Little Sip (Helen), and Sip (me)—were enough for our parents to handle. Helen was a small, dainty child, always neat and tidy. Mother could dress her in a white lac ʳ dress on Sunday mornings, and at the end of the day her dress would still be spotless and beautiful. I could never understand that. By each day's end (and Sunday was no exception), my own dress was usually filthy, stained, and sometimes torn from fighting or climbing fences with my older brother. My hair, worn in three long braids, would be matted with leaves and dirt, my face smudged and sometimes scratched.

Poor Mother must have been grateful for Helen's delicate ways. Lemuel and I were—well, a bit precocious and maybe at times mischievous. I was allowed to talk back to Daddy whenever I wanted. I could sit on his lap and smart-mouth as much as I pleased. Our exchanges went like this:

"You did."

"I didn't."

"You will."

"I won't."

"It is."

"It isn't."

I even called him black and ugly. Mother never played that game with me. I suppose she never learned the rules.

Daddy and I both knew the rules of our game. Although we teased, neither of us for a moment doubted the unconditional love and the unqualified regard that we shared for each other. He had nice features, a smooth complexion the color of rich, dark chocolate, and sparkling white teeth, two of which were tipped with gold. He was of average height and rather portly. By age fifty he was almost completely bald and not at all self-conscious about his baldness. When he lathered his chin and cheeks, he just kept on going to cover his entire head with shaving cream. After shaving his face and dome, he splashed both with shaving lotion. He said that nature had offered him the choice of either hair or brains. To him a cleanly shaved head was a fashion statement—and, I suppose, an intellectual manifesto as well.

The beauty of Mother's youthful years lingered her entire life. Sometimes when the family traveled by train, conductors would insist that she move to the "for whites only" area, misled by her light and clear complexion. Occasionally she moved to avoid a scene. More often, though, she created a scene, and usually won the resulting argument. It seems that she had little use for that particular game either.

ADA LOIS (FRONT RIGHT) WITH NEIGHBORHOOD CHILD AND CHURCHWOMEN

Daddy pastored the little church in Chickasha under Bishop E. M. Page. His first promotion above the local level of ministry came in 1930, when Bishop Page named him superintendent of the southwestern Oklahoma district of the COGIC. His jurisdiction covered churches in Oklahoma City, Lawton, Chickasha, Duncan, Anadarko, Pauls Valley, and several other towns. His duties were to oversee and appraise the fiscal and spiritual operation in the churches. His authority was to commend or censure pastors for their leadership. In 1935 Daddy was promoted to the position of the state business manager and later state bishop of Oklahoma. Even before these later appointments, however, he was highly respected within the denomination. Errant ministers feared his displeasure more than any sanctions that he could officially impose upon them. Although he was thoroughly Pentecostal, I never once heard him speak in tongues. Neither was he given to a shouting style of worship. Rather, he was a biblical scholar and a professional manager who commanded respect by his own hard-won achievements and his solid, rocklike character. No one—not his fellow ministers, not the folk of his congregation, not the white people whom he encountered—no one ever referred to him as "Travis" or "T. B." You addressed him only as "the Reverend Sipuel," "Bishop Sipuel," or "Dad Sipuel," the latter being reserved for his fellow ministers and those closest to him.

Because of his wider duties, Daddy traveled regularly to the twenty or so churches under his jurisdiction. Weekends were usually spent at home, where he prepared his own sermons and kept up with the paperwork for the denomination. In time, I became something of his unofficial secretary, who did his typing and helped him draft letters and reports. Even before then, however, much of my own life revolved around the church. We kept the sabbath day not only holy but busy, starting with Sunday school, following with the eleven o'clock service, continuing right through afternoon YPWW (Young People Willing Workers) activities, all topped off by Sunday night services and prayer meetings. Many Sundays ended with the three little Sipuels curled up in church pews, sleeping away our exhaustion until Mother and Daddy would awaken us to go home, where our own beds lay ready for us.

With Daddy away much of the time, Mother directed and guided our upbringing. She was rather tolerant of Lemuel's and my youthful misadventures; Helen never had any. They say that Lemuel cried when he learned that his first sibling was a sister. He had wanted a brother, so he proceeded (with little resistance from me) to turn me into one. I grew up a tomboy who followed my brother to school and throughout the neighborhood, joining in his misadventures and occasionally getting into my own.

Brother and I enjoyed lying on the grass and watching large white cumulus clouds form and drift away as the wind blew. It would be fun, we thought, to drift with the wind, going any place we liked without asking. We decided to run away and be free to go and see the world. One midmorning we quietly packed a sandwich each and some cookies and sneaked away. I was four and thought this would be great fun. Brother and I followed the railroad tracks. We felt adventurous as we walked the rails about ten blocks to the edge of town. Soon we were hungry and found a boxcar on a side rail. We sat down in the shade beside it and ate our food. We then realized we had no water or other drink—besides, we were still hungry. We decided to abandon our adventure. If we hurried, we would be home in time for lunch. We trotted much of the way and arrived in our backyard just as Mother made the lunchtime call. We were winded but no worse off for our misadventure. Mother never knew. That remained our secret.

Daddy did not condone corporal punishment. He tolerated a child's receiving an occasional swat from Mother, but everyone else in the church, school, and community knew not to spank or strike the Sipuel children. Our love and respect for him was sufficient to keep us on good behavior—at least while he was home from his travels. One day, though, after repeated warnings from Mother, my misconduct exhausted her patience, and she decided to spank me. An apology or promise to behave probably would have ended the matter right there, but I was stubborn and would rather take a spanking than give an apology. Instead, I ran to Daddy for comfort and (I hoped) protection.

"How many swats?" he asked.

"Four," Mother answered.

"Okay," he said, "I'll take them for her."

He did, while I squatted in front of him, peeping at the entire procedure.

Mother was a generous, loving, protective parent. She was young in spirit and could relate to many of our concerns and youthful situations. There were two things, however, that she would not tolerate. One was lying. "Tell me the truth when you do something wrong, and I may spank you; but lie to me and it will be just like killing snakes." The one other thing that she could not abide was being "simple." A simple person, in Mother's eyes, was not necessarily unintelligent, but failed to think critically and use good judgment. The worst thing she could say of anyone—even one she did not care for at all—was that he or she was simple. When she met up with a liar and a simple person, both were sure to suffer her wrath.

One hot day in July when I was five years old, I persuaded Mother to fire up the big wood-burning kitchen stove and bake a large gingerbread. I had an insatiable appetite for gingerbread, and Mother often made it for me, but it took a lot of love for her to do that in the sweltering Oklahoma summer heat. She gave Lemuel and me large slices of warm gingerbread, poured us tall glasses of cold buttermilk, and sent us to a pallet spread under the big shade tree in the backyard.

I considered Lemuel the smartest person alive; after all, he was in third grade in school. If he said something was true, I believed it. Lemuel saw a chance too good to miss.

"Lois, would you like to know how to have all the gingerbread you want for the rest of your life?" he asked.

"Yeah," I answered. "How?"

"Well, don't eat your piece. Instead, take it over next to the fence in that bright, sunny area, dig a good deep hole, and plant it. When you wake up in the morning, you will have a large gingerbread tree."

Of course, I believed him, and of course, I did it.

"Now pour your milk over it to wet it down."

Down went all the buttermilk, soaking into the freshly dug dirt.

Mother had been looking out the window. She was upset by what she saw and came out to investigate. "Lemuel," she said firmly, "that was a bad thing you did to your sister. I'm going to spank you."

She and Brother started toward the house. When they reached the porch steps, she turned and looked at me sitting under the tree, crying over my disappointment. "Lois, you come on too," she told me. "I'm going to spank you for being such a fool."

I may have been many things since, but I have tried to make sure that being simple was not one of them.

Generally, though, Mother tolerated a great deal from Brother and me. We learned early that for most mischief we would be counseled. Punishment was rare. Perhaps that is why I remember so vividly the one time that we got in serious trouble for cruelly pestering an old man who lived several blocks from our house. Poor Mr. Martin had to walk past our house to get to the railroad tracks and follow a shortcut through the freight yard to get downtown. Lemuel and I, on our way to the theater, came up behind him. The old gentleman had one crippled leg and walked with short staccato steps, maintaining the beat with the tapping of his cane. We moved close to him and began to clap our hands in rhythm with his steps. Then we sang in synch:

> *Mr. Martin went a-fartin'*
> *to get a bail of hay.*
> *Mr. Martin came a-fartin'*
> *blowed the hay away.*

We taunted the poor old gentleman all the way to Main Street. He continued his syncopated journey without once reacting or confronting us.

Several hours later, we arrived home and found a thin hickory switch lying across the kitchen table. No one offered to take the punishment for us.

....

The economic structure of our community was typical of African American communities of the period. For all the talk of a New South, employment opportunities for blacks were limited. At the top of the socio-economic structure were teachers, ministers, and a few professionals. Three men in town claimed to be doctors, but only one, W. A. J. Bullock, was able to write prescriptions for regulated drugs. The others used patent medicines and foul-smelling home remedies. There was one dentist, Henry Pruitt.

Ranking just beneath that group were people like the Harris or the Argo families. These were small business operators (Mr. Harris ran a general store and Mr. Argo kept an ice plant) who ran their enterprises behind segregation's walls. There were a number of others businesses, including a funeral parlor, a cleaning shop, two barbershops, and a taxi company that ran two cabs. There were also a drugstore, several restaurants, barbecue houses, and beer parlors. At different times there were about six grocery stores. As in most communities there was an unadvertised but not unknown "red light" district, its name identifying yet another form of enterprise. Chickasha was unique for its size in that during the 1920s and 1930s it had two black-owned and -operated movie theaters. One, the Hayden Theater, was about a half block from Lincoln School, Chickasha's African American comprehensive school. It featured mostly the old silent cowboy films. Cowboy films were more popular than romantic ones, probably because they had more action and the audience could get more involved. During one film in which Tom Mix was being overcome by a crook, an inebriated patron became so excited that he leaped from his back row seat, raced down the aisle, pulled his knife from a boot, and cut the screen trying to hurt the bad guy. About 1928 Mr. Joe Hayden sold his equipment to Mr. Albert Hilburn, who opened Hilburn Theater on what is now Ada Sipuel Avenue. At that time it was Idaho Avenue. It operated five or six years until Mr. Hilburn died.

Some African American men worked for the railroad, and a few worked at the cotton gin and compress. Almost always, they held the lowest-paid and most physically demanding jobs. Young men worked at filling stations. Other jobs were more irregular: janitors, yard workers, and bootblacks. A few families owned small farm acreages outside of town. None produced commercially, except for small amounts of cotton.

Cotton may not have been king in this so-called New South, but it still exacted its tribute in labor. Young adults and school kids as young as nine or ten chopped cotton in spring

FLOSSIE THOMPSON'S PIANO STUDENTS.
HELEN MARIE SIPUEL IS SECOND FROM RIGHT, FRONT ROW;
ADA LOIS SIPUEL IS FOURTH FROM LEFT, BACK ROW.

and picked cotton in late summer and fall. I used to see them waiting in groups at street corners, laughing and joking. A large, open-top truck would stop and pick them up in the mornings. When the trucks came by our house just after sunrise, they would be singing and waving. It seemed such fun that I sometimes wanted to cut school and go with them. I never did—at least in part because I noticed that there was not nearly as much singing and waving when they made their way back just after sundown.

Most of the women worked as cooks and maids. The job requirements included not only the ability to cook and clean but also general skills in taking care of "their white families." Because there was no bus service, maids walked to work. A fortunate few were transported in the back seat of their white ladies' cars. Most did not have uniforms. They wore freshly starched aprons with sturdy, low-heeled shoes and carried large shopping bags. I was always curious about what was in those shopping bags. I remember that the maids uniformly seemed to have soft voices and pleasant, smiling faces.

My mother was one of the few women in the community who did not work outside the home. Only once did she even try. One of the church women kept telling her about the fine, Christian white lady that she had once worked for. "Mrs. Sipuel," she would say (no one outside of her best friends and immediate family ever called my mother by her name, Bell), "Mrs. Kelley is so nice, and she does need help so. I've told her all about you. Won't you please go over and talk with her?"

Eventually Mother agreed to take the job. She walked up the front sidewalk, climbed the steps to the sprawling porch, and rang the doorbell. At first Mrs. Kelly apparently thought Mother was white. Mother then identified herself as being sent to inquire about a job as a maid.

"Are you Bell?" Mrs. Kelly finally thought to ask.

"I am Mrs. Sipuel," Mother coldly answered.

She then entered the house to hear Mrs. Kelley explain the job to her. She would cook and clean and wash and iron and sew and mend . . . and, of course, she was expected to come by way of the back door, like the rest of the colored help.

As many times as I heard her tell that story, Mother never told me what her own answering words were. In fact, she sometimes ended it by saying that she lasted one day, sometimes that it was a half day. Either way, Mrs. Sipuel never darkened Mrs. Kelley's door (front or back) again.

Our family did not suffer by Mother's not working outside the home. She worked hard enough at the church, in the community, and in the home. She was a good cook and enjoyed making cookies and pies for her always-hungry brood. Daddy drew a regular salary from his own church and another and larger salary from his state positions. From time to time the grownups would talk about something called a "depression," but we children hardly knew that there was one—or even what the word meant. I suppose by today's definitions and expectations we were somewhat deprived; but I do not remember poverty. As youngsters we had everything we really needed and most of what we merely wanted.

Lemuel had a large, shiny bicycle, and Helen and I always had dolls. From earliest childhood we owned our own home and a car (one of very few privately owned cars in the black community in the 1920s), as well as a telephone, a radio, and other items considered luxuries at that time. We also had a lot of love and a very close-knit family.

By all contemporary standards, the Sipuel family was among the town's black families who lived well. For many years the Harris and Sipuel families had the only telephones on the east side of town. People from eight and ten blocks away would come to our house to make a telephone call. Wealthy white ladies would call our number to contact their maids for a day's work or to tell them to pick up a load of laundry to be done in the maid's home. Mother always sent us hurrying. Sometimes the women would give us a cookie or a piece of gum, but we were never allowed to accept money for delivering the message. "These people need the money to support their families; they don't need to be giving it to you," Mother told us.

Ours was also one of the few families to have a radio set on East Dakota Avenue. For that reason, our front yard became something of a community social center. Particularly on warm summer nights, neighbors would bring their chairs and set them out on our lawn. Mother would open one of the front windows and turn our large, console radio to face it. Every-one's favorite broadcast turned out to be "Amos and Andy." None of the adults thought it at all inappropriate to laugh at the foolishness, shenanigans, mispronunciations, and just plain ignorance of the characters, who were, of course, portrayed by white comedians. Then, neither did any of us think it odd that we automatically rooted for Tarzan to slay the savage natives while we watched movies from the balcony of the segregated theater downtown.

Our family's comfortable lifestyle did not allow us to put on airs, though. Like other families in the community, we tended a vegetable garden, raised chickens, and kept a family cow for milk. If she did not do any white woman's laundry,

Mother did our own. She did it every Wednesday, and she did it like every other black woman at the time. The procedure was always the same. She built a fire under the large, black iron pot that squatted on three short legs in the backyard. Making several trips to the well and carrying a large bucket in each hand, she dumped a hundred pounds or so of water into the pot. When the water was hot, she scooped it into buckets, carried them to the shady side of the house, and poured the scalding water in galvanized washtubs. Then she scrubbed our clothes by hand on washboards, rinsed them in two or three tubs of clear water (each tub filled by hand), starched them thoroughly, and hung them on long clotheslines to dry into stiff boards. A few hours of work over a pair of hot irons (called sad irons), one heating on the wood-burning stove while the other pressed our garments, brought Wednesday's labor to a welcomed and exhausted close.

Our house was large by the community's standards, but no one would have mistaken it for a palace. We were warmed by the large wood-burning range in the kitchen and a potbellied cast-iron stove that sat on a large protective metal sheet in the living room. At night the fires were allowed to burn out and the embers to cool, and gradually the house would grow cold. In extremely cold weather, Mother would place warm, thickly wrapped sad irons in bed with us. Thin, dry twigs of wood, paper, and matches neatly lay at a safe distance from the stove. This enabled Daddy or Mother to quickly heat the living room and kitchen the next morning before their brood must crawl out of warm beds and run across cold bedroom floors. Every house had smoke pouring from the chimneys. Mostly the smoke was gray, but if coal was being burned, the smoke puffed thick and black. To me it had a rather pleasant, pungent odor.

What Chickasha's whites may have regarded as an undifferentiated "colored town" (assuming that they had used that particular term) was known to its residents as two rather distinct communities. The earliest African American settlement was west of the Rock Island railroad tracks and ran to the south edge of town, about sixteen blocks. Later arrivals, like my family, settled east of the railroad tracks. For many years, First Street on the west side was the only paved street in either community. The only paved sidewalks were on the west side too. They lay a half block along First Street and along two sides of Lincoln School. Other streets would get muddy and messy when it rained. Since there was no bus service and only two taxicabs, almost everyone walked in the street for lack of sidewalks.

Some families on the east side had pens out back and kept two or three hogs for family use. A few—ours was one—also owned a cow, and some had one or two horses. On both sides of town people raised chickens, ducks, and geese. Nearly everyone tended a vegetable garden too. There was often a backyard swing and a pet for the children.

As late arrivals and an east side family, we had a large fenced backyard with a chicken house, a smokehouse (which doubled as a playhouse for Helen and me), and a pigpen, where we raised two hogs each year. Until the early 1930s, African Americans in Chickasha did not have city water in their homes and used backyard wells as their water source. Some families did not own their own well, so they were always welcome to use those of their neighbors. With no plumbing, everyone had an outhouse set far back on the alley. Some were better and more sanitary than others. Ours was one of the best. It was a deluxe three-seater with two windows and a latched door. It was well maintained and equipped with a barrel of lime and old magazines. (I did not see store-bought rolls of tissue until I was well into school.) We quickly learned how to crumple and squeeze magazine paper until it was as soft as tissue. Sometimes neighbors would borrow the use of our magazines and one or two of our holes. Of course, Mother never objected.

....

Take a seat on the front steps of the school or the First Baptist Church on a Saturday afternoon, and you would see at least one member of most community families walking south from downtown to the residential area. Passersby usually carried one or two large, brown grocery sacks and a pair of pants or a dress that they had picked up from the dry cleaners. Everyone spoke and was friendly. A lot of adults had at least one gold tooth or crown in the front of their mouths. Men chewed gum a lot and whistled as they walked.

The depression years promoted a strong sense of community. Neighbors helped each other. You could always drop by a neighbor's house for a bag of fresh greens, okra, green onions, or tomatoes. You were welcome to go into the large garden to dig a few potatoes and were sometimes even given salt pork or pork skin to cook with the vegetables. Anyone who needed could send a kid to borrow a cup of sugar or cornmeal. Usually the borrowed items were not returned, but later you borrowed eggs or such, so on the whole it evened out.

I suppose it was that swapping process that made it all a community, whether it was east side or west side. I know that in my neighborhood, if the wind was blowing and the odor of fried chicken, meat loaf, or tender greens reached a certain neighbor, her grandson would come to the kitchen door with a plate: "Grandma said would you please send her some chicken and greens" or whatever. It did not seem preposterous at the time. People shared. Looking back, the entire African American community was a kind of extended family.

Like every family, we had some eccentric members of our neighborhood. One of the most eccentric was an old woman who lived nearby. Grandma Wilson had a son and grandchildren who lived in the neighborhood, but she was "Grandma" to all the children for blocks around. She lived in a tiny, two-room house two doors west of us. The kitchen was always tidy. The living room was also the bedroom. It held a large brass bed, which must have had several mattresses, a large, round, wood-burning stove, and several old but comfortable cane-bottomed chairs. The house had a front porch precisely the same width as the house. Such houses were called shotgun houses, presumedly because one could stand in the front door and fire a shotgun straight through the whole house and out its back door.

Outside were a wire fence, several pots of multicolored moss, and some rose bushes. Grandma always kept a bucket of rags burning during summer evenings. The smoke kept mosquitoes away. We knew that smoke always followed the ugliest person present, so each kid would subtly shift from place to place so as not to be in the direct path of the smoke.

Grandma knew of every possible form of ghost, ghoulie, wraith, and apparition. She told us how she was born with a veil over her face—and we never doubted it. Her beautiful, silvery white hair was almost waist length and was braided and pinned in large chignons on either side of her head. She was the first person I had ever seen with pierced ears and small, gold loop earrings. Her gingham dresses were ankle length, and she always wore a large, beautiful apron. She dipped snuff and kept her small snuffbox in her apron pocket. The old lady across the street ate dirt. Not any dirt—only hard, clean, red clay. Grandma did not eat dirt. She just dipped snuff and kept a small, dry twig of birch close by to stir the snuff in the can.

On her front porch Grandma Wilson had an old slat-bottomed chair piled with two or three faded pillows. She sat in that chair as on a regal throne. All the youngsters sat around her on the floor. She told us of large pumpkins that floated high up in the darkness and sometimes fell to the ground as great globs of jelly. We knew to watch out for those globs of jelly when walking in dark areas at night. We also knew that anytime we felt a hot blast of air we must cross our fingers, for we had encountered a ghost. She identified several old abandoned buildings in town as haunted houses. If you watched closely on dark rainy nights you might see eerie lights floating past their windows. We were never allowed out on dark rainy nights. That may be the only reason that we never got to see the lights.

Our parents often knew without asking when we had visited Grandma; there would be the pungent smell of coal oil on our breath. She was something of an apothecary as well as a "seeress." Her remedy of coal oil and sugar would not only cure colds and sniffles, but would also protect against unfriendly spirits. To cure arthritis and most organic illnesses, she prescribed a copper penny to be worn on a string around the ankle. Serious viral and bacteriological infections demanded stiffer remedies: wild broom weed brewed with a bit of corn whiskey.

Sometimes Grandma Wilson would drop by for a brief visit. If by chance we were eating, she would usually refuse Mother's offer to sit and eat with us. "I'm as full as a tick," she would say. Then she would stand and survey the table and often have a change of heart. "On second thought," she would allow, "I believe I will eat just a bite." By the end of the meal she would have eaten as much as or more than the rest of us.

Since nearly all of us kids called Mrs. Wilson "Grandma," I guess we must have felt some kind of extended-family kinship among ourselves. If so, it was an often strained kinship, full of rivalry of the sibling and every other sort as well. One reflection of this was what we called each other as nicknames.

Back in those days, many whites, and not only Mrs. Kelley, insisted on calling black people by their first names. If that name was unknown to them, they might call them George or Jane, any old name, as though African Americans had no individual identities. Of course, black males were commonly and generically called "boy" and females "girl," right up until their old age, when they were magically transformed into "uncle" and "auntie." I have often thought that that may be why African Americans tend to give their children unique and creative names or use initials with their Christian names; it asserts a special identity while discouraging whites from calling them by whatever common name comes to mind.

In a similar way, nicknames were common in our black

community. Such names usually began in childhood and continued into adult years. To this day, when someone telephones and asks for "Sip," I know that it is someone from my growing-up days. In my hometown about half of the black residents had nicknames, which give an insight into the collective personality of the community. These nicknames often related to the person's physical appearance, personality, or lifestyle. My siblings and I, of course, were Big Sip, Sip, and Little Sip. Our friends included the following: Peanut Patty, T-Bone, Dudie-Wink, Jaybird, Paddlefoot, Biff, Alley Oop, Whoopie Do, Ducie, Hitler (a woman), Pretty Mama, Fuzzy, Pretty Papa, Big Jim, High Line Slim, Footsie, Poppa Jack, John Do, Juice (Lemons), Skeeter, Fruit (Orange), Shakey, Yellow (a fair-skinned girl whose name was pronounced to rhyme with "Jell-O"), Bookie, State, Mutt, Cool Papa, Hoss, Tombstone, Weezil, Beanie, Boo, Sonny Man, Scooter, Tee-Tang, Soddie, Nuggin, Deedlum, Big Head, Sweetie, Tiny, Kutchie, Big Cuz, Bush, Hoghead, Sugar, Dallas Red, Boo-Low, Nina Mine, Big Hand, Dinner Bucket, Hammerhead, Blood Weed, Bass, Kong (as in King Kong), Red, Wildcat, Panther, Dickie, Dago, Sweet Milk, and Molasses (who became 'Lasses and eventually Syrup; the owner answered indiscriminately to all).

However odd the nickname, no one responded to one as an insult. It was just part of growing up. In the same way, no one took offense during one of our popular games: playing the dozens. The "twelves," as some called them, carried a strong rhythmic beat as kids competed to fashion insults about other kids' ancestors. Mothers, grandmothers, and other female kin were most frequently referenced. Some dozens rhymed; others did not. In one classic form, the dozens' taunt began with "Yo' mama," followed by a barbed insult about the target's wealth, morals, or looks, as in "Yo' mama so po', she kicks a can down the street and sez it's movin' day!" Properly done, the response would be something like "Yo' mama like a do'knob—everybody gets a turn!"

Competition could take physical form as well. Before I

started to school, Lemuel taught me some skills I would need to survive: how to throw and block punches, step back, and move in. I was not as strong as the first- and second-grade boys that he and I fought along the railroad tracks in the evenings, but I was fast and I had good instincts. I could help my brother a lot, and I did, right up until he outgrew his need for me as a partner. By the time he had boys his own age to pal around with, I was able to take care of myself—and was ready to do so. From third through about sixth grade we used to fight a lot during the walk home from school. Sometimes fight partners and combatants were decided on during the noon hour or the two-thirty recess period. Threats, dares, double dares, and double-dog dares (the last never to pass unchallenged) began during those periods and carried over to the walk home.

Youngsters left school in bunches. Each bunch had its regulars. Our bunch was made up of second- to fourth- or fifth-graders who lived east of the railroad. We walked down First Street one block to Idaho, then east several blocks to the railroad tracks. There some proceeded east and others turned north. As soon as we were out of sight of the teachers, the action would start. Each person was honor bound not to tattle to parents or teachers.

When I was in the fourth grade I learned the hard way that fighting girls was different from fighting boys. I got in a fight with a classmate, Clara Hayden, and she beat me up. We had prearranged the time of the battle, and a large group of fourth-graders formed a tight circle around us. I threw the first punch and prepared for a short, hard follow-through, when to my surprise and horror, she lashed out and scratched my face! What kind of person would use long fingernails to scar and injure another?

I hit her hard, high on the cheek, and grabbed for a stranglehold to wrestle her to the ground. She ripped again and again, easily drawing blood. I finally got her down on the ground and pinned her arms. By then I was hurting and ready to compromise. Mercifully, some of the onlookers pulled us apart. I claimed victory and hurried away. After that humiliating encounter I knew how to fight girls. It was a lot harder than fighting boys. I regained confidence, and while I did not start fights, I did not run away from one either.

Because I was a minister's daughter, I had more than my share to confront. Everyone seemed to think that preachers' kids were fair game, safe targets because they were not allowed to do things that other kids did. Those who teased me found out differently. "Be careful what you say to me," I would warn them. "My father may be a preacher, but I'm not."

Probably because I was so obviously unwilling to turn the other cheek, verbal sparring never developed to the point of physical conflict again until I was in the sixth grade. Then one day, while the home economics teacher was out of the room, one of my best pals, Norma Lee Porter, and I got into a fight—not scratching and squealing, but honest-to-goodness punching, hitting, and kicking, with some strangleholds thrown in toward the end. I think I surprised her with my strength and skill. When someone yelled, "Here comes Mrs. Williams!" we backed away, and Norma promised to finish it later. We still have not finished it, but we were soon best pals again.

....

During my growing-up days there were no playgrounds or parks for African Americans. There was a large city park— Shannon Springs—but of course it was for whites only. Black children found fun things to do in family yards, at the end of dead-end streets, and even along the railroad tracks.

Among my favorite fun things were trees. Almost every house I can remember had at least one large shade tree, usually with a bed of large red ants making their home in a mound near its trunk. With no home air conditioners and few electric fans, a large tree was almost a necessity during hot Oklahoma summers. There were some fruit trees, but even their primary utility was shade.

A popular tree in my neighborhood was in the backyard of Mrs. Wilhelmina Richie. It was not uncommon for several families of birds to nest in the giant cottonwood. The tree shaded a large area where a croquet diamond was always in use and youngsters lined up to await their turn at the game. Our only other regular playground was in the unpaved streets. Because there were only a few automobiles in the black community (and because whites rarely drove through it except to transport their maids), most warm afternoons saw the streets transformed into crude baseball diamonds, where both boys and girls learned to play the game.

Another of my favorite fun places was a large, leafy mulberry tree in Mr. Rufus Bell's front yard, around the corner and a block down from our house. The berries were large and sweet. They turned a bright red before maturing to a deep, rich purple.

Mr. Bell forbade us to climb his tree, not because he really cared about the berries, but because we would sometimes break branches. We took his forbiddance as a challenge, and it had a predictable consequence: up the tree we would sneak and chomp, chomp. Sometimes the front door would open and Mr. Bell, seventy-plus years, would step out. We would stop moving, curl around a branch, and lie perfectly quiet. Most of the time the old man was on his way to Harris's neighborhood store, and we could resume chomping as soon as he rounded the corner. Sometimes, however, he would take a seat on the front porch, bite off a chunk of chewing tobacco, and sit and rock for a while. We would then have to scramble down and hit the ground running. It was every child for himself, and you had better not fall down because no one was coming back to help you. While the old man was still shouting and waving his arms, we would turn the corner and be out of sight. He never pursued us.

Persimmon trees were also wonderful. They were usually a mile or so out of town on back roads. Lemuel and I knew where many of the best trees were. We would walk the distance and gather a bucket of the fruit, which was a bright, orange color but not yet ready for consumption. We had to wait for frost to cover them. To bite into a persimmon before it was ripe was a bad experience, probably like getting a mouth full of alum. We would place them on top of our barn and await a heavy, white frost. As soon as one came, we scurried up the tin-roofed structure, straddled the gable, and devoured juicy persimmons. This was a special treat. Sometimes we carried some to the house for Helen, Little Sip, who remained too clean and ladylike for such fun.

Kids found their fun wherever they could. In a vacant lot not far from our house a man often staked his horse to graze on the high grass and weeds that grew there. It was an old, swaybacked, gentle horse. Lemuel and I would sometimes join two or three older youngsters and pay the old nag a visit. One of us would hold the rope and bridle while the others used a box to climb on for a ride. One day when it was my time to lead the horse around and around the stake, I got tired of pulling the rope and hit the horse with a good-size stick. The old horse suddenly took on some life, bucked, jumped, and dumped the riders to the ground. We all ran away. Two of the group had stiff backs and sore behinds for a few days. I doubt that we bothered the horse anymore after that experience.

....

In all of these ways, the children of our community managed to grow up. Like our parents and other adults, we lived behind segregation's walls, and we lived as best we could. Ours was a simple life with rewards that easily transcended a sore behind here or a swiftly forgotten tussle there. The grownups had their own lives, with their own challenges and their own rewards. Both testified to their remarkable abilities to cope with the world as they found it, a world that they managed to warm with fantastic, creative skills.

Sometimes that literally meant warming. These were the

depression years, years in which African American adults found it difficult just to heat their homes. Fuel for heating—like money and other needed commodities—was scarce. Through the early 1930s the primary fuel source was wood. Coal was preferred because it burned longer and hotter, but coal was expensive. Occasionally the Rock Island railroad would switch their freight cars to sidetracks overnight to await the arrival of other freight that would complete the full load to be shipped to some distant destination. Sometimes these were flat, open-top cars of coal that sat near the station or the roundhouse, where equipment was stored and repaired. News of the location of the coal car would swiftly spread through the east side and near west side, and coal hustlers would quietly prepare their strategy. They knew schedules well enough to know when work crews clocked out for the day. As soon as the last worker left for home, the hustlers would descend. Through the night men would carry large canvas bags of coal on their backs from the rail lines to their homes several blocks away. Some even maintained their own private storage bins: predetermined stash places near the rail line. All through the night we could hear the traffic moving. A dozen strong, fast men working five or six hours could unload and carry away a large amount of coal.

So certain and so great were the losses that the Rock Island would sometimes assign guards (called "bulls") to watch the cars overnight. Swiftly regrouping, the hustlers responded by hiding in ditches and bushes. When the morning conductor flagged the engineer to move out and the train started rolling, the coal men would climb aboard and proceed to pitch or roll large chunks of coal over the side. They would work until the speed of the train was fairly fast and then jump off. Wagons, wheelbarrows, push carts, and every conceivable mode of transportation would race along the right- of-way, picking up the coal.

Because the success of the operation depended largely on compatibility, there were few conflicts among the hustlers. On the contrary: theirs was a business in which private entrepreneurs agreed to cooperate to share and expand their market, kind of like a miniature black National Recovery Administration. If so, it was more effective than the one that ran out of Washington. For several days after the haul their business boomed, as carriers would sell coal by the tub or sack full at very affordable prices. For a couple of weeks or so our stoves burned brightly and thick black smoke poured from chimneys.

Some of these men were so brazen that they raised their entrepreneurial efforts to an art form that earned them a certain degree of respect in the black community. One was particularly famous, for he had a big family and a large, barn-like house that required plenty of fuel to heat. When his supply ran low, he would just drive his mule and wagon up to the coal storage bin at night, lower the chute directly into his wagon, and load up. The story is told that on one occasion the fellow so overloaded his wagon that his mule could hardly pull it. "Get on away from here," he shouted. "You know you done pulled bigger loads of coal than this."

The railroad was utilized in another way. Young men, both African American and white, who were unemployed and unable to find jobs, would "ride freight" to other cities looking for jobs. They would hide inside empty freight cars and go wherever the train was going. This was a national phenomenon. North, south, east, and west they went. The men knew the junction points and final destinations of many regular runs. Railroad bulls tried to keep these hoboes off the trains. To avoid them, the riders would wait in nearby bushes until the trains started to move, then quickly scamper aboard and hide in dark boxcars. If all car doors were locked, they would lie flat on the top of the cars as the train raced forward at high speed, the wind whipping their hair and clothes about. They generally returned several weeks later just as penniless as when they had left but with interesting stories that made them momentary celebrities to the community.

One man, Jasper, was acknowledged and respected as the best train hopper in town. Jasper's feet turned inward a bit, and he walked and ran with slightly rounded shoulders. Posture and style notwithstanding, Jasper had world-class speed. People said he could walk almost as fast as other men ran. He would run alongside the moving train until it reached a relatively high speed, then grab a handle, climb a few rungs, and fling himself to the top of a boxcar. He would then walk atop the fast-moving train, jumping easily from one car to another, until he found an open door or a sheltered flatcar. It was almost impossible for the bulls to catch him.

Jasper was also known, even admired, for his ability to elude the local cops. In fact, some regarded him as something of a hero in the Robin Hood tradition. Jasper never stole from his neighbors or other African Americans. But he did steal coal and everything else from trains, warehouses, and everywhere else. When the police got after him, he just ran. The chase was a much-admired contest of both wit and speed. Jasper ran down streets, up alleys, across backyards, and even through people's houses if their doors were unlatched. He could be hiding under your house without your knowing it.

If Jasper was ever caught and arrested, I never heard of it. I did hear that he moved to another state after a close call for breaking into train cars loaded with furniture and clothing. He returned for visits twice, his presence known and respected in the black community. Still regarded by some as a hero, to the police he was just a fugitive.

The community had its other heroes who, like Jasper, gained respect along with notoriety for their toughness, talent, and imagination. One such legendary hero was Matthew Odom. Not nearly as swift as Jasper (either physically or mentally), Matthew was legendary for his strength. His fame was permanently sealed when a white circus played in town. One of its featured attractions was a wrestling match in which a bear, old and nearly toothless, went up against some local talent. In Chickasha that was Matthew, who entered the ring, grabbed the bear around the middle, and proceeded to almost squeeze the life out of the flailing animal. Disaster was averted and Matthew's status secured when the promoter screamed out, "Fella, let go of that bear! You're killin' my livelihood!"

Nearly as famous as Jasper and Matthew were the two Johnson brothers. Both were law-abiding citizens, in fact, deacons in their church. They did believe, though, in protecting their property. On one occasion they did so by firing a shotgun at a man they found sneaking around their backyard pigpen. The man was unhurt, but he demanded that the police arrest the two. Montis Adams, the white sheriff's black deputy, went to bring them in. He did—in a way. The Johnson boys were driving the wagon that pulled up to the Grady County courthouse with Deputy Adams securely leashed to its rear.

No more successful were the cops that decided to raid an old woman famous among both blacks and whites for her home brew. Prohibition was the law. Bootlegging was the consequence, and this woman was said to make some fine stuff. In fact, she was mixing up a batch in a tub when the cops broke down her door. Instantly, she pulled the tub in front of her chair, sat down, and stuck her bare, unwashed feet in the foul-smelling liquid. While the cops searched everywhere for contraband, she went on soaking her feet. They finally gave up and left. The old woman thereupon removed her feet, dried them on an old rag, and proceeded to pour the tub's contents into quart fruit jars. Neither the police nor the customers ever knew the difference—except possibly for the improved flavor of that particular batch.

Chickasha was a tough town, and the African American population took pride in its toughness. The black athletic teams (sports, like everything else, were thoroughly segregated) took special pride in that reputation. Doubtless, they benefited from it too. Our school's football and basketball teams regularly won championships, as much for their opponent's fear of beating them, it was said, as from their own athletic skills.

If so, the fear was not misplaced. Old-timers still recall how

Douglass High School, Oklahoma City's all-black school, dreaded to play us at home. After nearly every game, the Douglass folks would find themselves stranded in hostile territory, the natives of which had cut the tires from their cars. On one notable occasion, a Douglass running back streaked across our football goal line, where he confronted a crowd of well-armed toughs. The Douglass boy immediately turned tail and ran the other direction, his way unimpeded by either team. The local scorekeeper then took the six points from their side of the scoreboard and transferred them to ours.

It may be that black Chickasha's reputation for toughness reached a national audience. I know that the folks who grew up there still brag about the time that the Harlem Globetrotters came through town to play an exhibition game against some of our local boys. It turned out to be one of the few games that the Globetrotters ever lost. It seems that they had a remarkably bad shooting night. Their unaccustomed errancy was perhaps not unrelated to the presence of thugs who stood under our basket, guns conspicuously at their sides. Those local fellows must have been prophets too, because when they told a Globetrotter, "You gonna miss that shot," the player usually missed.

Shots were not the only thing the Globetrotters missed. When the team left our gym to board the bus for their next barnstorming stop, they found it sitting strangely low to the ground. Some of our boys had missed the game, spending their own time taking the wheels—tires, rims, lug nuts, and all—right off the bus.

....

I may be guilty of nostalgia as I look back over those times, but I do not think so. In some ways, it was a good time and a good place to grow up. What I feel now is less nostalgia than pride. My mother, my father, my brother, my sister, and I built a strong and happy family, strong enough and happy enough to give me the roots and the shade that I found so long ago in those old trees.

I have found there resoluteness and comfort many times. For that I take pride because from that I took nourishment. I took it from my family, from our community, from our school, and from our friends and neighbors, from people who never for a moment let us think that we were anything but special.

In their own way, they were special too. It may not have been the kind of special that shows up in the history books that I later used as a college student or professor. In them, you might find the name of Henry W. Grady, and you might find a chapter on the New South. What you will not find are Jasper and Matthew and the Johnson boys. Neither will you ever see Dallas Red, Alley Oop, Dinner Bucket, or Molasses (in any of his incarnations). In some ways, those books are still like the park at Shannon Springs: for whites only.

I still see them, though. I see them now as people who inherited a world that men like Henry Grady only pretended they could mold. Such men were wrong. The Chickasha, the Grady County, and the New South that I knew were the creations not of the distant and the prominent but of the present and the unacclaimed. The signs may have said, "For Whites Only," but their other sides said nothing.

What we put there was our own creation. It was put there in the handwriting of Mr. Bell and of Grandma Wilson and of Dr. Bullock. It bears also the penmanship of Bishop T. B. Sipuel, whose daughter, Ada Lois, challenged the "For Whites Only" side. It bears the mark of the ice dealer Dan Argo, whose son, Henry, was the only person lynched in Chickasha.

SEPARATE BUT EQUAL

··

During my growing-up years, my hometown, its surrounding county, and the entire state of Oklahoma were but a short step removed from their frontier days. We still had living examples of the pioneers who first settled the area. Almost every family had stories of how rough times had been when their parents or grandparents first arrived there. These stories treated their ancestors as heroes who wrestled the elements of frontier living: breaking ground, living in dugouts or primitive cabins, harvesting first crops, building schools, churches, and other institutions of civilization. They helped tame the Old West.

Often the stories included tales of outlaws, bandits, and criminals whose ends finally and fairly came at the end of vigilantes' ropes. A good number of these bad men were said to have been horse thieves. By one estimate, Oklahomans lynched thirty-four of them in just eleven years, between 1885 and 1896. Many years later, people looked back on those days with no small element of pride. Justice, it seemed, was another of those things in short supply in the Wild West, and their parents and grandparents helped bring it there by the only means possible. It added to their heroic stature.

The frontier passed, but the stories lingered. In time a second category of stories joined them. These were not stories of the Old West but of the New South. The central characters were not righteous vigilantes and despicable horse thieves but lynch mobs and their victims—men, women, even children, whose only crimes may have been that they were black. In African American communities, those stories were told and remembered.

There was the story of Carl Dudley, a black man who got into a shooting scrape with white policemen in Lawton, about fifty miles southwest of my hometown, in 1916. He died with his back to a wall, his head torn to pieces by at least fifty bullets, fired by members of an unmasked crowd. Later the mob dragged his body through the streets of the black section of town and left the mangled corpse dangling from a telephone pole.

Closer to home was the lynching of Bennie Simmons. Charged with the rape and murder of sixteen-year-old Susie Church, Simmons was entrusted to the Caddo County sheriff and placed in the county jail. A mob of one thousand removed Simmons from the jail, carried him to a wagon bridge, and tied him to the limb of a tall cottonwood tree. Coal oil was poured over his body. According to the newspaper accounts, Bennie Simmons prayed and shrieked, but the yells and jeers of the mob drowned his screams. When his cries grew fainter, the mob realized that he was losing consciousness; then every member of the crowd emptied firearms into the swinging body, which was literally cut to pieces by bullets and buckshot. Bennie Simmons's body hung there for some time, suspended from a limb over the Washita River eighteen miles west of Chickasha.

Many black families came to Chickasha from towns such as Norman, Lexington, Pauls Valley, and other nearby towns. Most left their former homes, as my family had left Tulsa, because of racial violence. Some were fleeing towns, such as Norman, that officially (and legally) prohibited blacks within their borders after sundown. The Sipuel children learned about Dick Rowland, the destruction of Tulsa's black community, and my father's being tagged and held in a detention camp outside the city limits. Mother, often mistaken for a white woman, told us of being warned about "niggers."

When I was five years old, I heard the older kids and grownups whisper and murmur that something big and exciting was about to happen in our town. It sounded awfully special, and I ran home and told Mother about it. I wanted to get dressed up in my very prettiest dress—"Mother, will you fix my hair?"—I wanted to look my very best. "Lemuel, you and Helen, get your best clothes too! Haven't you heard? We're gonna have a race riot, right here in Chickasha!" I thought the older folks were talking about a big race—a horse race, probably—and I did not want to miss it.

Mother did not fix my hair, and my brother and sister did not get out their Sunday clothes. Instead, Daddy got out his old musket. That night we slept on pallets, curled low to the floor. Over us stood the adults of three families who were gathered at our home. Pooling their firepower, the men waited behind locked doors and drawn curtains, waited with shallow breath and cocked firearms.

The morning of May 31, 1930, was a beautiful spring day, and Henry Argo, a nineteen-year-old black youth, went fishing on the banks of the Washita River. Later that afternoon, a white deputy sheriff stopped him and two other young men as they were walking south out of town. What had happened in the hours in between is still subject to controversy.

What is known is that Mrs. Angie Skinner swore that Argo was the boy who had come by the Skinner family's concrete-lined dugout northeast of Chickasha that day and attempted to strangle her nineteen-month-old son before brutally raping Mrs. Skinner. Some African Americans said—and still say—that the incident was not a rape but one of numerous planned romantic encounters between Angie and Argo that was accidently discovered. Most people of both races later agreed that there was suspiciously little evidence of any crime at all. Angie Skinner's white neighbors who saw her ten or fifteen minutes after the alleged four o'clock rape subsequently admitted that she gave no sign of having been assaulted, and the Skinners' little boy bore no marks about his neck or anywhere else.

Those facts emerged later. At the time, a black deputy of Sheriff Matt Sankey identified the suspect as Henry Argo. Everyone in the black community knew Henry and his father, Dan. Dan Argo ran an ice plant at the corner of First Street and Oregon, and he did a good business in our community. Although he charged a few pennies more per pound to fill up the neighborhood's iceboxes, my family and others usually traded with him because he was the only iceman who made home deliveries. Dan Argo's short frame and potbelly were familiar sights in the African American part of town. Almost as familiar was his son, Henry, a slow-witted boy who had come from Arkansas the previous March to live with his father.

It was 5:15 P.M. when Sheriff Sankey placed Henry Argo in the Grady County jail. Within three hours a mob, estimated to number as many as two thousand men, had descended on the jail to attack its external doors and walls with sledgehammers, crowbars, and battering rams. By nine o'clock Adjutant General Charles Barrett had ordered the local National Guard unit to the scene. The militia arrived an hour later, and several speeches were made in defense of law and order. Likely more eloquent, however, was the cold, silent muzzle of the machine gun that the troops sat up on the jail's steps. That gun had to be more effective than the municipal police force, which calmly went about its business only two blocks from the courthouse. "This is county business," the cops said, as they continued to check doors, round up drunks, and ticket speeders.

It took about two hours (and probably a large amount of liquor) for the mob to get up its nerve again. The crowd attacked the jail a second time, seized the truck that had brought the guardsmen, and used a chain attached to its frame to remove the jail's badly battered door. Fighting continued inside the building between the National Guard and the mob until the mob set the jailhouse afire. The retreating guardsmen then carried away their own wounded (five of whom had been seriously injured) and all of the jail's prisoners—except one, Henry Argo.

Their way unimpeded, the mob set grimly about its task. After failing to break through the jail's solid iron door, the men took out chisels and hammers and began smashing a hole in the concrete side wall. They tired before the hole was large enough to permit anyone to enter, so about 3:30 A.M. someone fired a gun into the cell. A bullet entered the top of

Henry Argo's head and proceeded downward into his neck. Henry Argo slumped to the floor and began to die.

The mob enlarged the hole in the cell until, by morning, it was large enough for several spectators to enter the cell. One who did so was George Skinner, Angie Skinner's tenant-farmer husband. Mr. Skinner buried his knife in Henry Argo's heart, then went out on the courthouse lawn and collapsed. A sympathetic newspaper account ascribed Skinner's misfortune to "overtaxed nerves." He was taken to the local hospital, examined, and released. Miraculously restored, George Skinner bragged that he had only had to stab Argo once. "You know," the press reported him boasting, "I only have to hit a hog once."

Still clinging to life, Argo was transported to a facility in Oklahoma City rather than the local hospital in Chickasha. When he arrived at the Oklahoma City facility almost three hours later, he was dead. This was the last recorded lynching in Oklahoma. Some black families were said to have fled their homes to hide out along the Washita's banks; others stayed.

In time, a different legend evolved in the black community. We would recall the incident to be that Dr. W. A. J. Bullock, a pillar of the black community, had gathered a group of black men down at the courthouse, where they had protected Henry Argo for two nights, until Sheriff Sankey had persuaded them that the danger had passed. That after the lynching, the mob had threatened to drag Henry Argo's body through our part of town to teach us all a lesson. That Dr. Bullock had gathered together some bootleggers and gamblers—this was no job for church folks—and declared that any white man who crossed Minnesota Street with that boy's body would die in colored town.

Those memories, repeated for decades, say as much about my family and my community as does the lynching itself. I remember that Daddy often said later that no man was ever whipped by night riders that did not deserve it. Putting aside the circumstances of this particular atrocity, he would explain that any man that would let himself be whipped without killing some of his tormentors was not a man at all—he was a boy.

My father was a man. Dr. Bullock was a man. So were those tough, determined, black men that we remembered having protected us. The stories that we were told gave us these heroes, and they ensured that it was such heroes that we would remember from our people's pioneer days.

....

The Argo tragedy had consequences both short- and long-term. For a while Chickasha's so-called better class of whites admitted shame at the disgrace that the presumed lower elements had brought upon their fair city. The local newspaper, the *Chickasha Daily Express*, ran a few strong editorials about the need to maintain cool heads and to preserve law and order in such tense circumstances. Governor William J. Holloway and Attorney General J. Berry King announced that there would be thorough investigations. A grand jury was impaneled locally, and it returned indictments against George Skinner and twenty-two other men for assaulting Henry Argo and for "unlawfully, willfully, and maliciously and riotously set[ing] fire to and burn[ing] the county jail of Grady County, Oklahoma." Their trials were repeatedly postponed and eventually forgotten. The same fate apparently awaited the federal indictment that the twenty-three also had destroyed property belonging to the United States government—namely, the National Guard truck, which they had burned after using it to remove the jailhouse door.

There never was a successful prosecution for Henry Argo's murder. In time, the immediate sense of outrage and disgrace passed, but the experience left scars on both the white and black communities. It takes a long time for any town to get over something like a lynching. It took Chickasha a very long time indeed.

Other consequences came swiftly. Dan Argo closed up his little ice business, and the family left our community, eventually settling in Kansas City. In the Democratic primary held about two months later that summer, Matt Sankey, Grady County's sheriff and political "boss" for ten years, lost his job by a two thousand–vote majority. The newly elected sheriff pinned on his badge and instantly fired his black deputy.

Sheriff Sankey's defeat and his deputy's firing owed much to their rejection by both the white and the black communities. Unlike blacks in many other states, Oklahoma's African American population experienced no prolonged systematic disfranchisement. Probably every single one of Chickasha's estimated five hundred black voters voted to oust the sheriff. "Remember Henry Argo" was the slogan for most. My mother, however, had a different one, one that became the only political sign that she ever placed on a family automobile. "To Hell with Matt Sankey," it read. During the 1930s she became a major figure in Chickasha politics. In fact, she, Wilhelmina Richie, and Joe Price became something of a black caucus that interviewed, measured, endorsed, and supported candidates for the various local and county offices. Because the rest of the community respected the group's integrity, candidates had to respect their ability to carry the black precincts. In every election, political aspirants sought out their support. During campaign seasons the candidates provided Mother and her group money to buy and put up posters and to hire cars and drivers for election day. In time, mother became such a political force that when her parking meter downtown expired, the policemen and deputy sheriffs would often put the change in for her rather than write her a parking ticket.

Mother was able to get the first asphalt road on the east side of town. In those days, Oklahoma's county commissioners spent considerable sums building roads, their location determined less by drivers' needs than by the local commissioner's political needs. Although these were supposed to be outlying roads in the rural areas, Mother managed to convince one commissioner that his own political interests lay closer to home—to our home, that is. The result was a half-block-long stretch of asphalt that ran from the railroad track before making a sharp turn on East Dakota Avenue and ending at our front door. "Sipuel Road" was its informal name.

The Argo incident may have been one of the things that brought my family closer to Dr. Bullock. A squat bear of a man who nearly always had a foul-smelling pipe nearby, Bullock was one of the most admired men in Chickasha. Respected by the town's white civic and business leaders, he was seen as a dependable bridge linking both sides of town. He was also one of the few professionals, something of a role model as well as protector. He was the Sipuels' family physician, the man who could be counted on to walk over to our house at any hour of the day or night to attend a sick child. He walked because he did not own a car until very late in his life, and even then, he could hardly have been said to have driven one. Rather, he kind of pointed it and trusted to the Lord—or to the alertness of other drivers.

Dr. Bullock was the man who organized and directed Chickasha's chapter of the National Association for the Advancement of Colored People (NAACP). I still vividly recall the time—I was in the seventh or eighth grade—when Dr. Bullock brought an NAACP representative to speak at Lincoln School. The speaker was in the state as part of his work, which included helping small chapters all over the country. In the main, though, he was a lawyer, only the second black lawyer I had ever seen. I remember seeing this one because he was the most handsome, articulate, brilliant, and charismatic man I had ever seen. Our speaker's name, Dr. Bullock told us in introducing him, was Thurgood Marshall.

Mother was active in the local NAACP branch, and she saw to it that we were exposed regularly to its magazine, *The Crisis*, which was edited by the legendary W. E. B. DuBois. We also read the *Chicago Defender* from time to time and other "race newspapers," including Oklahoma City's marvelous weekly, the *Black Dispatch*. Daddy was too busy with church work to get actively involved. He gave us, however, a very valuable political lesson, one that drew on his own religious heritage. He did not teach us that we were as good and smart as whites. On the contrary, he taught that we must remember that whites were as good and smart as we were.

....

Nobody who grew up in a place like Chickasha in the 1920s and 1930s had any doubt that we were different. Before and after the Argo lynching, the white community persuaded itself that the city was something of a model of race relations in the New South style. Whites and their black neighbors got along just fine. After all, the "colored" folks knew their place.

If we did not, it was hardly for lack of instruction. Like the city park, Shannon Springs, the municipally-owned zoo, swimming pool, and golf course had big signs that read, "For Whites Only." After the close of the last black-owned silent movie house, black people entered the one movie theater, the Washita, by way of an outside fire escape that led to the balcony. After it closed, we went into the main entryway to the new theater, the Ritz; but once inside, we had to take the stairway to the balcony. We could buy candy and pop in the lobby, but the water fountain and restrooms had the familiar signs. So did just about every place that we went downtown, including the city hall, the Grady County courthouse, and the United States federal post office.

No one bothered to put up signs on the public schools, since everyone knew that they were thoroughly segregated. Oklahoma's schools had been segregated even before statehood. The constitution of 1907 absolutely forbade the mixing of races in the public schools. In racially diverse Oklahoma, the constitution's authors were careful to declare that any person of any degree of African American ancestry was to be regarded black while "all other persons"—Indians—would be deemed white.

Only in the last regard did Oklahoma vary at all from the southern states, which routinely segregated schoolchildren. In one constitutional feature, though, Oklahoma was unique. Its fundamental law directed that the dual school system would be financed by completely separate tax mechanisms, one tax base and rate for the white schools, other "separate but equal" ones for the black schools.

Of course, those three words are among the most famous ones in the long history of American race relations. Enshrined by the United States Supreme Court in the infamous *Plessy v. Ferguson* case of 1896, the doctrine of "separate but equal" long provided the legal excuse that voided the Fourteenth Amendment's plain demand that no American state could "deny to any person within its jurisdiction the equal protection of the laws." Under this legal fiction, the south—including Oklahoma—proceeded to require separate public facilities in public transportation, education, and just about any conceivable point of possible human interaction. In Oklahoma this eventually included a state corporation commission order that directed telephone companies to provide "separate but equal" pay telephones, I suppose to eliminate the threat of intermixing the nickels of callers.

However irrational that particular form of segregation, as practiced in the public schools, it was hardly silly. Every southern state claimed to offer separate but equal education to the races, but it was a lot more separate than it ever was equal.

Oklahoma's peculiar constitutional school-funding provision all but guaranteed that the schools would not be equal. With the two school systems tapping different tax resources at different rates, any equality of funding would have been entirely accidental. The people who ran Oklahoma's schools were not about to allow that kind of accident to happen.

Thus it was that the city of Chickasha maintained as many grade schools for its youngest white pupils as did all of Grady County for African Americans of all ages. Chickasha had five elementary schools in its different wards. Grady County had a total of five black schools, four of them one-room, one-teacher operations outside the city school district's limits. The fifth was the one that I attended, Lincoln School. Although white Chickasha complemented its five grade schools with a junior high school and a fine high school, our

Lincoln School was comprehensive, educating about 530 or so pupils in all twelve grades in the 1930s. Only about 100 of these were in the high school grades, and of those, only about 10 or so graduated each year.

At the time, Chickasha spent about forty-seven dollars per year to educate each white pupil, nearly a third again as much as the thirty-seven dollars it was spending on the black students. That money allowed Lincoln to hire thirteen teachers. Each taught an average of forty-one pupils, using textbooks, globes, maps, Bunsen burners, and even classroom desks and chairs that came down second-hand from the white schools. It is amazing that they taught so well.

My first contact with Lincoln School was at about age four, when I would accompany my brother to his second- and third-grade classes. The wooden seats were wide and heavy, with a broad desk bolted to heavy iron legs. There was ample room for two small children to sit and write. I accompanied him through third grade before I was eligible to enroll as a regular student. I went with Lemuel, carrying my own thick nickel tablet and penny pencil. I also carried my brown-bag lunch. As the older children learned the alphabet and numbers, I also learned.

Teaching was an esteemed and prized occupation for African Americans. Jobs were hard for black women to come by, and most could do no better than provide poorly paid domestic service to their "white families." Teaching was one of the few professions open to women, and we seemed to have attracted some of the very best and most ambitious of them.

My first-grade teacher was Mrs. Florence Daniels, a kind, white-haired lady who was skillful in dealing with five- and six-year-olds. She was spry, always walked rapidly, and brooked no shouting or shoving in her classroom. Students who misbehaved were either paddled or placed in a semi-isolated supply room.

I might have been prone to misbehave even had I not been able to read and write when I began school. Watching Mrs. Daniels teach other students things that I had learned before I enrolled bored me and gave me idle time. As it was, I was sent to the supply room pretty often. I resented even a few imposed minutes in the quiet area. When ordered there, I would sometimes go into wild temper tantrums, falling on the floor, yelling, kicking, and spitting at the teacher and other students. This could go on for five or ten minutes, however long it took for Mrs. Daniels to ignore me and direct the attention of the students elsewhere. When I lost my audience, I would gradually wind down and, dirty and rumpled, eventually be released to my seat.

One day, during a particularly intense tantrum, the laughter and shouting of my classmates suddenly stopped. The silence was ominous, and my intuition alerted me that something must be awry. I looked up into my mother's upset face. She yanked me up and escorted me out of the building and three blocks home without conversation. I knew I was probably in trouble. Unfortunately for me, Daddy was out of town that day, so Mother and I settled the matter her way.

There was one youngster who sat several seats behind me in second grade. Though well-mannered and quiet, the boy slept and wet almost daily in class. Others in our row in front of him would feel wetness underfoot, look around, and our boy would have his mouth open, sleeping and relieving himself. Sometimes the stream ran all the way down to the front of the room.

I suppose the poor boy eventually outgrew that problem. I was in the third grade before I outgrew the temper fits. I still had my behavioral problems. Namely, I remained headstrong and smart-mouthed. Of the two, the smart mouth kept me in difficulty most often. It still does.

Back then, my smart-mouthing often was my ticket to the office of Lincoln's principal, Robert Goodwin Parrish. It seems that I punched that particular ticket quite a few times. We talked, no paddling. Lemuel also had his share of learning experiences in Mr. Parrish's office. The surprising thing is that Helen, so demure, so delicate, and so ladylike, once got there by succumbing to the Sipuel smart-mouth gene herself.

Parrish was a tall, handsome, extremely dark man with a full head of hair that showed only the first signs of graying. He was a forceful, highly gifted, effective speaker and a superb teacher. In most respects, he reminded all three of us very much of our own father. Both shared not only similar emotional and intellectual qualities but (beneath the hair lines at least) similar physical ones as well. Both had the same complexion, size, and build.

It may have been those similarities that led to one of Helen's few troubles at school. One day Mr. Parrish's youngest daughter, Helois, and my little sister, Helen—both first-graders—got into a fuss and shouting match. At issue was what turned out to be a justly fighting matter. The two little girls were trying to settle the claim of which had the daddy who was biggest, blackest, and baddest. The argument was never resolved.

Many of Mr. Parrish's students might have been prepared to let Helois take the honor. Quite a few of my fellow students found his personality intimidating. I did not. I enjoyed engaging him in conversation and argument about almost any subject. Later, I was happy when he picked me to compete with the Lincoln School debate teams, which he coached. Luckily, our debate topics never included the relative bigness, blackness, or badness of our community's men.

Although it has been more than fifty years now, I think that I can remember every one of my teachers, from grade school on. I am sure that their pay was never equal to the town's white teachers', and they could have had no illusions about the equality half of the separate-but-equal formula as applied to equipment and facilities. Nonetheless, they were remarkable people who regarded themselves less as separate than as special, and they were determined that we would be that way too. Even though I was valedictorian of my class in 1941, every one of my classmates was secure in the belief that he or she was a special person, a beneficiary of what our teachers (and others) made of an unfortunate situation: a tragically separate but very special upbringing.

LINCOLN HIGH SCHOOL GRADUATION, 1941.
ADA LOIS IS FOURTH FROM LEFT, SECOND ROW.

One of my favorite teachers was Cash Black, an excellent English teacher and also a good coach. He and his wife, Bennie, were a youthful, warmhearted couple. Many of our group would flock to their house for good food and soft drinks. I think maybe his influence led me to major in English as an undergraduate in college.

I also remember Jennie Baker, Johnnie Pearl Coffey, Lizzie Stevenson, and Geneva Edwards as the glamorous fashion ladies of the faculty. They were excellent teachers as well. My mathematics and science teacher was T. O. Rogers. Lincoln was not much given to overspecialization, so Mr. Rogers added to his science and mathematics instruction the duties of directing our school band. In that regard he was a generalist, for Mr. Rogers could play almost every instrument in the band. Initially our little band wore white pants, shirts, and shoes. It was 1940 before we had anything like the uniforms of the city's other high school band. In 1941 we got beautiful black-and-gold outfits with braids and plumes.

I enjoyed music classes from the elementary grades on. Mrs. Eva Boyd was our music teacher. As soon as I reached junior high I tried out for the school choir and became a

THE LINCOLN SCHOOL BAND, CA. 1939. ADA LOIS, THE ONLY FEMALE TO PLAY
TRUMPET, IS FOURTH STUDENT FROM LEFT, SECOND ROW.

member. By my junior year I was one of several soloists in
the choir, and I was also a member of the a cappella group.
We took the entire world of Western music to be our domain,
with special pride in the operettas that we regularly performed for our parents and the rest of the community. The
highlight of each musical year for us came every Christmas
season, when the Lincoln School choir would present George
Frideric Handel's *Messiah* for the entire African American
community. Mrs. Boyd was a counselor and confidante as
well as a teacher.

Every so often the (all-white) board of education would
request that a small group of us perform as a prelude to their
monthly meetings. A trio or small choral group would be ushered into one of the downtown restaurants, where the board
held luncheon meetings. It was the only time that we entered
those businesses, which "reserved the right to refuse service." Usually we would do the two or three songs especially
requested for the meeting and be ushered right back out.
Almost always, the requested numbers were Negro spirituals,
which the board members favored. "Swing Low, Sweet
Chariot" and "Go Down Moses" were especially popular.

Once a year the board of education came to us. Because a single, elected board governed both school systems, its duties included oversight of both the seven white Chickasha schools and the one "separate but equal" black school. As far as I could tell, the one manifestation of that responsibility was the board's annual "inspection" of Lincoln.

The visit was announced well in advance; the teachers and students cooperated to have the facility spic and span. Red oil restored some of the luster to the old, worn wooden floors. Windows were washed, and the broken ones would be replaced. The blackboards also got a good scrubbing and fresh, dark paint applied to conceal their worst cracks. Even the flat, old felt erasers got their once-a-year cleaning, the kids beating them against rocks to remove the accumulated chalk dust.

By the time the board members reached us there was not a hint of dissatisfaction or a suspicion that there was cause for any. On the contrary: we would convert the two-room home economics department into a banquet hall, our old, long tables transformed by borrowed lace cloths and adorned with some family's best crystal and silver. Just before the noon visit, the second-floor halls would fill with the savory aroma of dinner rolls, fried chicken, and other delicacies.

Through the lunch hour, students kept the halls clear and tried to keep the classrooms quiet while the board members and their wives feasted. Afterward, there were furtive glances into the open doors of classrooms they passed on the way out and a good-natured quip or two with Principal Parrish. A few gouges at their teeth with wooden picks signaled the close of that year's inspection and the discharge in full of the school board's duties.

I suspect that most of Chickasha's white school and civic leaders were less devoted to the academic quality of our school than to the prowess of our athletic teams. I am certain that they were more interested in them. Our hallways might creak and groan in their cries for repair, but the basketball court was always well tended and its floor always glistened.

While the band was still wearing plain slacks and shirts, both the basketball and football teams sported fancy black-and-gold gear, including warmup suits.

The football team could not play on the field at the white high school. Instead, our teachers and coaches marked off an open area at the county fairgrounds with white lime. Unconfined by stadium seats, the spectators stood on the perimeter to urge our boys on. If one of them broke away, the entire crowd would run along the sidelines to keep up with the runner. If one of the opponents got loose—like that poor Douglass boy did—he had better hope that the toughs did not get to the goal line first.

I was five feet, eight inches tall and very slender during my high school years. That meant that I was taller than many of the girls and even some of the boys in the group. I was never bothered by my height; it allowed me to play basketball by my sophomore year. They still called it girls' basketball back then, and we played by girls' distinctive rules. The competition was six on six, each team fielding three purely defensive players (guards) and three purely offensive players (forwards). Each unit was restricted to its appropriate half court.

I was a guard. The other two guards, Eva Ladd and Thelma Sanders, were equally tall, and we formed an effective defensive group. We were strong and had a reputation for being competitive. We were so aggressive and physical that our coach used boys from the male team during practice play so as to spare our offensive teammates injuries.

Our offensive teammates were equally good. From 1939 through my graduation year in 1941, Pearl and Juanita McDonald, Alva Baker, Evelyn Smith, Vivian Sneed, and Claudia Wilson were outstanding forwards. We truly loved our experienced and innovative coach, Mrs. Bertha Fletcher. Her teams always scored high in tournaments; her Lincoln team was usually the team that everyone wanted to beat, although not many did.

Our coach also demanded good academic performance, loyalty, and sportsmanlike conduct. Just before games we

ADA LOIS'S SENIOR CLASS
PICTURE, 1941

would suit up and sit on the floor of the locker room to hear her final admonitions. Before hard games, she built our confidence by reminding us of our demonstrated ability. "You are all good players and trained athletes. Play hard—but play fair and clean."

Pumped up by her words, we responded: "Yeah! Yeah! Mrs. B. We're ready! Bring 'em on! Let's go git 'em!"

Then she would look directly at me and say, "Don't get caught, Sipuel. Just don't get caught."

Other than fouls on the basketball court and smart-mouthing, there really was not all that much to get caught at. Drugs and alcohol were known to us almost exclusively by reputation. We heard that some shady musicians smoked something called marijuana, but none of us even smoked tobacco. It was a tradition, however, that during the last week of school seniors would drink beer. We were so unaccustomed to it that a single glass would put some of us on the floor.

Outside church and athletic activities, our primary place to hang out was John's Café. It was located about a block from the school at a point where most youngsters walked on their way to and from school. Pop and potato chips were five cents each, and fifteen cents would buy you a large, greasy hamburger. A neon-lit jukebox stocked a score or so hit tunes, each of them available for a nickel. The variety ranged from slow ballads to jumping jive—just about everything except country.

After basketball games and other evening activities, we would crowd into John's, throwing down the burgers and pop and playing the jukebox. Soon music would be blaring and John's old floor would be shaking under the impact of so many dancers. One of our classmates, J. R. Brown, always drew attention (if not envy) for his singularly muscular form of stomp dancing. The fellow was heavy-set and had very large feet. The two qualities combined on one occasion. While the boy was showing his most awesome moves, an entire section of floor caved in beneath him. John's survived with a repaired floor. The boy did also, his reputation permanently fixed.

....

Boys, clothes, and such did not occupy much of my time or thoughts in my preteen years. I was all of twelve before I thought of wearing red lipstick and silk stockings. At thirteen, when I asked my mother's permission, she agreed with the stockings but refused the lipstick. Eventually we compromised with bright red fingernail polish.

For most of my school years the only boys I paid much attention to were my brother, Lemuel, and the one I called my other brother, Warren Fisher. I first saw Warren when I was a small girl. He was the new boy in town, the youngest son of the Reverend T. F. Fisher, a Baptist minister and pastor of the Second Baptist Church. I was about seven years old; my sister Helen was five. Warren was around fifteen.

He was tall and slender, with a rich, copper-toned complexion and nice features. He had the most unusual eyes I ever saw. Khaki gray most of the time, they seemed to change colors with his moods. The range was all the way from a warm, burnished copper to cold, gunmetal gray. He had slightly dark lips and a strong chin, with a beautiful, expressive mouth that could quickly break into a contagious grin.

Warren and Lemuel soon found that they had common teenage interests in tinkering in general and fixing up old bicycles in particular. My parents liked him immediately as a bright, well-behaved, intelligent youngster. Mother eventually claimed him as her boy. He often ate with us and joined Lemuel in outdoor chores. In time, Mother and Daddy came to depend on him for many things. He drove the family on summer vacations while still a teenager. When Lemuel was old enough, Warren taught him to drive, and Lemuel took over part of the driving. Before long Warren was a regular member of the family, eating and sleeping at our place as often as his own.

Looking back, Helen and I admit that we both had a crush on him. In those growing-up years, we acknowledged both Warren and Lemuel as our brothers, people we could rely on: brother—and the other brother.

When you are seven and a fellow is fifteen or sixteen, your worlds are far apart. There is a definite generation gap. Even though it is less than a generation's span, it is at least the depth of one. I was a grade school girl, still a tomboy. Warren was a young high school man, popular with both his teachers and peers, especially the female ones. I remember some of his girlfriends. He always had plenty, and most of them were beautiful young ladies. I liked them, and they liked me. Some often called me little sister or play daughter. Sometimes I would carry notes and little messages from them to Warren. They frequently gave me a nickel or chewing gum for my trouble.

Life was fun. Life was good. In time, it developed that there were a couple of junior and senior high school boys that I liked. My first date was when I was fifteen years old. I was a sophomore and not really interested in any fellow for a boyfriend. Luther Wimberly, a popular and handsome senior, stopped me in the hall at school and asked me to be his senior prom date. I was surprised, and Mother agreed. Jesse W. Draper was a classmate whom I dated for about a year and a half. "J." was my first steady boyfriend. Lemuel and Warren accepted the fact that, at sixteen, I was growing up and dating was okay. They kept their eyes and ears open as to the status of my social life, however. Besides, they were old enough and experienced enough to know that high school crushes often end when high school is over.

Theirs certainly did. During and after their own high school years, both of them became accomplished lady chasers—and more than fair lady catchers too. In those days, kids often had a particular song that they associated with a special romantic interest. Mine was Hoagie Carmichael's "Stardust." Lemuel's romantic theme song must have been "O Come, All Ye Faithful." If they came to him, he was not the faithful one. Warren, who looked very much like Lemuel, was just as handsome as he—and just about as faithless. Those two chased, caught, and moved on so regularly that Mother and Daddy had to put a back door on the house so the two of them could come and go without awakening the rest of us at all hours.

By the time J. and I were seniors, Lemuel was in college at Langston University and Warren had left Langston to go into the army, stationed at Fort Sill, in nearby Lawton. Warren had a lady friend whom he visited on the weekends. The girl was one of several "play moms." One summer weekday just after my graduation she made me a wonderful offer. It seemed that her mother was going to be out of town, and she would be in the house alone all night. Would I like to bring J. over for a little private time? Would I!

J. and I made our plans and showed up at the appointed hour. The girl chatted for a bit, then picked up her purse and said she was going to a bridge party. She said we should make ourselves at home; she would be back in a couple of hours. We took that to mean that we should have a good time, and we prepared to do so. The lights were low, the music was soft, and we were swaying to the music—when I heard a key turn in the door lock. Thinking that it was just the girl returning to pick up something, J. and I kept the music low and our bodies swaying. Then the lights came on.

Warren Fisher was standing there, his eyes their very coldest shade of gunmetal gray. J. did not have much to say, so I tried to explain for both of us. We were not doing anything, really we were not. Besides, Warren's own girlfriend had said it was all right.

"I'll deal with her later," he said.

The words probably did not catch up to J.'s fleeing back as he left the house. Warren then loaded me into his car, started the engine, and headed for home. I sobbed and wailed, knowing I was in a situation much worse than when I threw the tantrum or taunted poor Mr. Martin. If those had earned me switchings, this one would have to deserve a club, at the very least. Warren drove, his lips as tight as the fingers by which he held the steering wheel.

Finally, we reached my house. Warren stopped the engine, and I continued my sobbing.

"Lois?" he finally asked.

"Yes," I timidly choked out.

"Lois, do you promise that there was nothing going on?"

"No, Warren. I swear."

"Have you ever done anything like this before?"

"Oh, no. Of course not. Please believe me."

"Well," Warren said, "I guess I don't have to tell your mother this time." Then he added, "If I ever find out that you're doing something like this again, I'll tell your mother about it and about this time too."

I gratefully accepted the amnesty. I did not question his motivation or how he came to have a key to his girlfriend's house.

I already knew that Mother put a lot of stock in Warren's word and judgment. I also knew that she was very protective of me. When I had been going to school, she almost never let me go out to the movies or other places on school nights. Somehow, though, if Warren happened to drop by and say that he was on his way to the show, Mother would always agree that I go along with him. Those were other occasions in which I did not think to question someone else's motives.

At the time, there was a lot that I did not think to question. Before the business with J. came up, Warren had stopped by our house fairly often when he came through from Fort Sill. He still had friends at Lincoln, so it was natural that I invited him to come to one of our school dances. He accepted the invitation and brought a nice-looking young woman with him. In gratitude, I assumed, he offered to dance with me several times. No girl particularly liked to dance with her brother, but Warren was a good dancer, so we danced a few times together. Once when I suddenly turned my head while dancing a waltz, I thought his lips brushed my face. No, I had to be mistaken. If not, well, accidents happen even in the best of families.

My high school beau and I went our separate ways and drifted apart. He went to Bishop College in Texas, and I went to Arkansas A & M in Pine Bluff on a scholarship. There I spent a pleasant first year away from home. Dormitory and school rules were rather strict, but I enjoyed singing in the choir and playing basketball. I went to campus movies, sometimes with girls and sometimes with two different young men who seemed interested. One was tall but too dull, the other interesting but too short.

During that year Warren and I exchanged letters fairly often. I told him things about my freshman-year experience. He seemed interested and encouraged me to hit the books hard and also to enjoy the available social activities. On my birthday the mail brought a lovely bottle of perfume from him. This, no more but no less than the letters and the advice, was typical of the thoughtfulness that I had grown to expect from my other brother.

During the summer vacation after my freshman year and before I would begin my sophomore year at Langston

University, I visited a girlfriend until dark one evening. I called home for someone to pick me up. Lemuel was out on a date in the car, Mother said, but Warren was there, and since the distance was only five or six blocks, she would send him over to walk me home. It was a beautiful balmy night, and we enjoyed the walk. We stopped and bought cold drinks. Conversation flowed smoothly about commonplace things.

About a block from home, Warren stopped, put his arms out, drew me to him, and quickly kissed me on the mouth. I was startled, angry, surprised, and scared. I had been betrayed by my friend and "other brother." I started to cry.

"I'm going to tell Mother what you did when I get home."

"Yeah, okay," he said. "Come on. I'm going to tell her myself."

Mother listened to my complaint and to Warren's quiet request that she and Daddy approve of his courting me. Her answer was that Warren should not have kissed me without my permission; however, she was giving him her permission to seek my hand. Daddy was out of town that day, but as soon as he returned he gave his consent.

I must have given my permission too, assuming that anyone thought to ask me and that I thought to respond. Within six weeks he had my heart. I was utterly, totally, madly, and permanently in love with Warren Fisher, and I knew that he would get my hand just as soon as possible. On Saturday, March 3, 1944, Warren and I married in a small, quiet ceremony in the living room of my parents' home; only the family was present. The next day I went back to Langston and Warren returned to Fort Sill. Shortly after that he was sent to the European theater of World War II.

After Warren finished high school in 1935, Mother helped with the cost of sending him to Langston University. When Lemuel finished high school in 1938 she could no longer pay Warren's tuition, so Warren joined the army. He would complete the baccalaureate work later. In 1938 the army was looking for and recruiting black college men to

WARREN W. FISHER AS A
YOUNG SOLDIER

fashion into a crack all-black field artillery group. Warren was placed in that group, the 349th Field Artillery, stationed at Fort Sill. The unit was designed and trained as a superior battalion that would train other field artilleries and white officers. Of course, it was a segregated unit, part of the army's own separate-but-equal structure. In this case, however, the separateness masked no inequality. If anything, the unit was one of the army's most highly regarded outfits. I do not know how many times Warren told me of the time that a visiting general, his cap and coat dripping with braid, took the boys out on the firing range for a demonstration drill and ordered them to fire at a target two or three miles away. Quickly after giving the order the general decided to change the target. "Too late," he was told, "the round is on the way, sir!" Instantly the target, miles down range, exploded. Thereafter, those last four words provided the unit's motto, proudly embroidered on the insignia patch and cap of every soldier in the battalion: "On the way, Sir."

From 1935 through 1944 the 349th was assigned to Fort Sill, where it served to instruct recruits (both white and black) at one of the army's largest field artillery schools. Our hometown was just about midway between the post and my campus, and Warren and I spent every weekend together after we married. We did not have a honeymoon. In fact, we spent the night of the wedding at my parents' home. No hotel or motel accepted African Americans, and there was no time to go out of town—we both had to be at our appointed places twenty-four hours later. Mother and Daddy had the good sense and subtle grace to leave us alone. In fact, I recall that they retired very early on our wedding night. Warren and I stayed up late, holding hands and talking nervously about any subject that either of us could come up with. It was nearly dawn before we exhausted the topics of small talk and got up the courage to go into our own bedroom.

As soon as we were married, I told Warren that I would be leaving school to be a better wife. His response was a growling "Hmpf!" followed by the declaration that I was to do nothing of the sort. "You're not going to stay married long if you don't get to school. I promised your parents that I would see to it that you completed your education, and that I would support you as far as you were able to go, and that's what I intend to do." So I went back to college and Warren went back to Fort Sill, where he immediately arranged to have almost all of his military pay allotted to me.

We saw each other as often and as passionately as possible. In so little time—it seemed like only a few weeks —Warren got his notice that he and the rest of the 349th were being shipped overseas. That was one dark day for me. I knew that he was a soldier, but I never had accepted the likelihood that he would ever leave me. Now he was, with a final training session at Fort Hood in Texas before assignment to the German Rhineland.

He was not long in Texas, just about long enough to call me and ask if I could afford to take off a week of classes to be with him. My instructors understood the situation, that I had good grades, and that I would make up the work. So I boarded a bus at its local stop (a café across the highway from the campus) and went to Temple, Texas.

Warren and I spent every possible minute with each other, as well as several hundred forbidden ones. For the last two nights, he was restricted to base, but he would manage to slip off to be with me, returning just at sunrise. In no time, the final day came. The unit was scheduled to ship out at dawn on a Monday—forget that I had to get back to class—and Sunday evening he told me, "You've got to go tonight, Lois."

Together we walked to the bus stop, hugged up so tightly that I do not know how we could walk. Every half block we stopped and kissed. I could not stop crying. Warren kept telling me, "Nothing's going to happen to me! I'll be back, and I won't be over there long. Don't worry about it. Don't worry about it."

In the pain of parting I was naïve enough to believe him, to trust that my Warren had some control over that. Finally I stopped crying. The nice driver felt so sorry for us that he held up the bus for a few minutes. Warren dried my eyes, and we got our last kiss in the presence of a bus filled with smiling strangers. The bus door closed. Warren turned and walked back to the base on his way to war. The bus pulled out and I headed north, on my way to Oklahoma's separate but equal college for Negroes.

....

I had spent one year at the school in Pine Bluff, Arkansas. At the end of my freshman year, Lemuel graduated from Langston University and went into the army. I then transferred to Langston, partly because it was closer to home, mostly because it was closer to Warren.

The college is located in Logan County, about twelve miles northeast of Guthrie, high atop an elevated mound of red clay known affectionately to its students and thousands of alumni as "the hill." The town, which is also called Langston, has an interesting history in its own right. Edward Preston McCabe, the black former Kansas state auditor, founded it as an all-black city just after the land run of 1889. Naming it for John Mercer Langston, a black congressman from Virginia during the Reconstruction period, McCabe hoped that the community would provide a physical nucleus of what might become a predominantly black state, Oklahoma. Of course, that never happened. The town's early growth—it boasted a population of two thousand in 1891—withered in the intense heat of racism, and the community barely hung on, its survival dependent largely on the presence of the "colored" agricultural and mechanical college that the territorial legislature placed there in 1897. Oklahoma may not have been predominantly black (its African American population remained steady at about 12 percent of the total from 1890 onward), but Langston, both the town and the university, were exclusively so. For the state's black residents, the school was the only state-supported institution of higher education available in Oklahoma. Of course, it was a state-supported separate but equal higher education, the most meaningful of all those adjectives being *separate*.

The town had a weekly newspaper (the *Western Age*), several churches, a couple of cafés (one of which doubled as the bus stop), and a grocery store. One of the few local businesses was a bookstore run by Mrs. George W. McLaurin. The wife of a Langston professor, Peninah McLaurin sold used textbooks out of her front parlor at very competitive prices. Unsuspecting students who purchased her books often learned that their low costs had a reason: the school had discontinued using them. That did not mean that Mrs. McLaurin discontinued selling them, only that she discontinued refunding the purchase price once the book left her parlor.

The town had no fire department or police force. There was a telephone service, staffed around the clock by a Mr. Wells. Anytime you picked up a receiver and turned the crank, Mr. Wells would answer, fast or slow, his speed depending on whether he was asleep or not. A late-night call might or might not get through. The odds increased proportionately to the operator's alertness. A daytime call might go something like this:

"Give me eight-six-four-six, please."

"That's Miz Jones's number, but she ain't home. She went over to Dorothy's house to get her hair done."

"Okay. Give me Dorothy, please."

"She ain't there now either. When Dorothy finished her hair the two of them went over to Guthrie to do some shopping. They probably won't be home for two or three hours. You want me to tell one of 'em to call you when they get back?"

Of all the inconveniences, the absence of a fire-fighting force was most dangerous. Unable to fight a fire, the college absolutely forbade any cooking or cooking equipment in students' rooms. The very existence of the rule only challenged us to find ways to cook without getting caught.

Most of us had hot plates. We heated cans of soup, chili, or pork and beans—with or without bread or crackers. The greatest challenge to our culinary creativity was not to attract attention by food odors. We mostly limited our entrées to things with little odor: fried or broiled eggs, wieners, and such. If we had money we would buy bologna and pork lard. If we had no lard we would make french fries with mineral oil. Once, in desperation, we tried cooking fries in Vaseline. That was a smoky mess. When we cooked fried foods we raised the old-fashioned windows and plugged in an electric fan. Hot or cold, rain or shine, the windows went up and the fan was on high speed. Once, when our hot plate was broken, my roommate and I took our electric iron and turned it bottom side up between bricks. We then poured a can of soup into a shallow aluminum pan and heated it up.

Male students had an easier go of it. Lawrence Cudjoe, a classmate and buddy, told me that he and his friends had a regular kitchen on their dorm roof, with a hot plate connected through a window to an inside outlet by a long extension cord. What we really envied were the guys' menus: rabbits, squirrels, quail, and fish taken from nearby fields and ponds.

One male student, Jerue Hawkins, became something of a campus celebrity, a chef famous for his frequent entrée of squab. In their living form, these had been pigeons that nested on rafters directly over the auditorium in Page Hall. Their fate was repayment in full for the many times that they had fouled the clothes or coiffures of the unsuspecting students who sat below.

Otherwise, food was no laughing matter. Bread was a common medium of exchange—a few slices of fresh Wonder bread would buy quite a few things. The food served in the college dining hall was good enough, but eating it required us to submit to the high-handed person who punched meal tickets. Fate must have cheated her. Not having been born in Germany, she missed her true calling in the SS, and she seemed to take out her disappointment on us.

Miss the 5:00 to 6:30 dinner period by even a minute, and you would be rudely turned away. Get there on time, and you still took your chances of being called foolish, dumb, ugly, stupid, or ignorant, the adjective of choice often followed with the "n" word. The slightest sign of resistance meant you might be refused admittance, ticket or no.

At that time, state jobs—including many of the most routine staff positions at colleges and universities—were thoroughly controlled through the patronage system. Prominent politicians (the district's state senator being the most likely figure) parceled out jobs to their supporters, both to display their power and to increase it. Thus the attendant was right when she told protesters, "White folks hired me, and these niggers here can't fire me."

Confronted with that reality, our strategy was a student boycott of the dining hall in 1944. In every dorm students pooled their money to buy large jars of peanut butter and jelly and huge bologna sausages. We bought up enough food to keep from having to go to the dining hall. Floor captains in each dorm handed out sandwiches three times a day. Out of around six hundred students, no more than ten or twelve went to the dining hall. Dining hall managers had to throw out large vats of prepared food. After four days the college officials worked out a compromise. Thereafter, an upper-class student worker punched tickets. Frau Whatshername stood close by, but she kept her opinions to herself. Of course, she kept her salary too.

Langston University had an outstanding faculty. Unlike the staff, faculty members earned their salaries by their abilities and energies, not by some politician's selection. They kept them by demonstrated commitment to education, and they provided an opportunity for an excellent one. The school's physical facilities were another matter. They were not much better than the evil Frau's attitude. At Langston I found the same pattern of neglect and inadequate funding I had known in public school in Chickasha and at college in Arkansas. The dormitories, classrooms, and administration buildings were old and outdated, as were the library and university auditorium. There were almost no sidewalks, and the ones that there were went from nowhere to nowhere else. Otherwise, there was only one paved spot on the campus. State Highway 33, which separated the school from the village, made a feeble branch off into a short stretch that ran to the door of the president's house and curved to exit at the northeast side of the campus. Otherwise, students prayed for no rain. Any downpour turned the hill's red clay into sticky mud, a form of cement that sucked a person's shoes off when he or she had to walk through it. Let a student get inside alive and still shod, and the mud would come off on the floors and carpets, drying to a red, paintlike substance.

It may have been the rain and the mud that did it. The spring of 1944, my junior year, was unseasonably wet and unreasonably muddy. Tired of the situation (and knowing the nature of Oklahoma's peculiar politics), a small group of students, including myself, decided that we would call State Senator Louis H. Ritzhaupt at his office at the capitol. The other students participating in that clandestine operation were Loise Young of El Reno, Thelma Reece of Muskogee, Velah C. Ross of Pauls Valley, William Gibbs from Waurika, Roger

Sutton of Okmulgee, and James Roy Johnson from Haskell. All were juniors or seniors, residents of Oklahoma, and leaders in student activities on campus. Ritzhaupt was a physician as well as the senator whose district included Langston. The problem was that we had no money to pay for a call, so we decided to place a free one. We slipped into the office of President G. Lamar Harrison while he was elsewhere and called the senator's office. We informed him that we would like to come to his office to discuss needed improvements at Langston. Instead, he offered to come to the campus to meet with us the next day.

When news reached the administration that a small group of students had summoned a meeting with the senator, we were called before the top university officials and counseled to be civil and courteous at the meeting. Senator Ritzhaupt, we were told, was a friend of the university. It would not do well to upset him. It certainly would not do well for us, for the university had ample punishments for students who undercut the administration's authority. I left the meeting fearful of my parents' response if I returned home, thrown out of school. Knowing them and considering the circumstances, I quickly put away those fears. Instead, I started praying: "Dear God, Please let it rain tomorrow. We need lots of mud when the good senator arrives."

The rain did not come, but Senator Ritzhaupt did. We were civil, and he was too. We were frank; he was also. He conceded that some improvements were needed. Still, all in all, he insisted that the facilities and funding for the university were adequate. Adequate? If only it had rained.

Since neither the Lord nor the senator had helped us, we resolved to help ourselves. Later that year the same group paid a visit to Roscoe Dunjee, the editor of the *Black Dispatch*. A student in the very first class to enroll at Langston, Dunjee had gone on to become one of the most prominent African Americans in Oklahoma or the nation. In the weekly columns of his *Black Dispatch*, Dunjee had written truth with moral lightning and righteous thunder. As an organizer and leading official of the statewide NAACP, Dunjee already had master-minded several lawsuits, two of which had reached the United States Supreme Court. The first lawsuit guaranteed African Americans the right to a trial by a jury of their peers, not a jury that purposely excluded blacks. The second affirmed their right to vote in Oklahoma by overturning the state's obvious and obnoxious subterfuge that violated the Fifteenth Amendment's suffrage guarantees. In other actions, Dunjee had fought (and financed) the actions that eliminated legally mandated residential segregation in Oklahoma City and elsewhere.

Roscoe Dunjee did not need us to tell him about Langston or about what needed to be done there. Nonetheless, we discussed with him our experiences—emphasizing the mud—and our hopes for improvements. He listened to our concerns intently and promised that something—he did not say what—would be done. We had no indication of what he had in mind. Still, we went away encouraged, thrilled just to have been there.

....

I graduated in May 1945. Back in Chickasha, I started collecting bulletins from the law schools at Howard University in Washington, D.C., and Northwestern University in Evanston, Illinois. A first cousin, Winston McGhee, was an attorney in Chicago. Everyone already knew I could talk. Maybe I could talk my way into a good law school, maybe even a job like Thurgood Marshall's, that NAACP lawyer who had so moved me in junior high school. I would wait a year to seek scholarships and save some money. Warren, who was still with the military forces in Europe, agreed with the plan. Besides, he might be home by that time.

One fall morning Dr. Bullock called Mother and said he wanted to talk with the family. He wanted to be sure that Lemuel would be there, since he needed to know if my brother was available for an important project. Dr. Bullock was still our family physician and was always a family friend. He had been to our home many times, usually responding to our phone calls. Of course, Mother invited him to come by that evening.

As we sat around waiting for his arrival, we talked about how long we had known Dr. Bullock. At least since the Henry Argo lynching, he had been the chief spokesman, role model, and protector of Chickasha's entire African American community. More than that, he had founded and for twenty-five years directed the local chapter of the NAACP. He also served as its regional director for southwestern Oklahoma. Neither Mother nor Daddy knew the specific reason for his visit, but we all sensed that it concerned an important or sensitive matter.

When Dr. Bullock arrived, we assembled in the living room. After a bit of chitchat, Daddy told him that since Lemuel had no inkling of the purpose of his visit, the doctor would have to spell out the complete scenario. Bullock did so, beginning with the state convention of the NAACP that had recently taken place in McAlester, Oklahoma, in September 1945.

There and then the state NAACP had heard Thurgood Marshall lay out a strategy to challenge segregated education at one of its most vulnerable points. If the separate-but-equal doctrine had any validity (and Marshall would not grant that it did), then it had to at least provide for separate educational opportunities for all races. Even if the equality side were ignored, then outright exclusion never could pass muster, even of the separate-but-equal sort. Well, Oklahoma provided a state-supported law school at the University of Oklahoma, but blacks could not attend it. They could attend Langston, but Langston had no law school. What Oklahoma (and several other states) offered was not even separate and equal. It was nonexistent, and it was wrong. Marshall was ready to kill the subterfuge of substantial equality. What he needed was a plaintiff, a black Oklahoman who was qualified to attend the state law school and would apply to do so.

Bullock told Lemuel that his scholastic records in high school and college were brilliant. Brother had a four-point grade average and had been a member of the President's

THE SIPUEL FAMILY, CA. 1943: TRAVIS B. AND MARTHA BELL (FRONT ROW);
ADA LOIS, LEMUEL, HELEN MARIE (BACK ROW).

Honor Cabinet his entire junior and senior years at Langston University. Bullock said the person the group sought had to have not only brains but also the willingness and ability to withstand a long and probably bitter controversy.

This was central to the plan, and no mistake should be made regarding it. After several years of protracted legal trials and great personal tribulations, Lloyd Gaines, who had been the plaintiff in a similar suit filed in Missouri, had mysteriously disappeared. Lemuel had to be aware of that. He also had to know that the plaintiff would have to be ready and able to commit to successful completion of the course of study at the University of Oklahoma. That meant study in Norman, a town legendary for its territorial pogrom, a town that still did not permit African Americans within its borders after the sun went down. The purpose of Dr. Bullock's visit was this: Was Lemuel ready to be that person?

Lemuel listened intently. Finally he spoke. He said he appreciated the offer, but explained that his education already had been interrupted for over three years. He had wanted to enter Howard University's law school when he graduated from Langston in 1942. Instead, he was drafted into military service. He had only recently returned from the war zone in Europe and been discharged from the army. Frankly, he said, he was now in a hurry. He wanted to get on with his education. Bullock understood. Daddy agreed, although he knew Lemuel would be an ideal choice.

I don't remember whether it was Daddy or Mother who suggested me as an alternate. I am inclined to think it was Daddy because he thought I was a smart young lady. He reminded Bullock that I was valedictorian of my high school class and an honor student myself at Langston. Mother and Lemuel chimed in, both declaring that I would be an excellent plaintiff. Besides, Mother pointed out, I was younger and only six months out of college.

As I recall, no one asked me if I was interested as a second choice. They really had no need to ask. As soon as Lemuel said no, I began hoping. When Dr. Bullock asked if I was available, I quickly said yes. The doctor reminded me that he could only recommend me; his personal choice was not tantamount to final selection. Other NAACP officers were looking about for probable plaintiffs in Tulsa, Idabel, Muskogee, Oklahoma City, and the other cities in which they lived. He had no way of knowing what other persons were being recommended as candidates by other officers across the state.

Still, I felt good about Bullock's acceptance of me. I knew my scholastic record was good and also that Bullock's recommendation would carry weight. As the doctor prepared to leave, we agreed to set up a personal meeting with Mr. Dunjee, president of the state conference of branches of the NAACP, as soon as possible. Bullock asked me to secure a copy of my college and high school transcripts. When he left the house, I danced around in little circles and clapped my hands. Lemuel stood there looking at me and laughing. Daddy was ready to declare that they had better select me, buttressing his manifesto with the boast that they could not find a better one. Had not he always told me I had a "big brain"? Now, he said, I may get a chance to use it in a historic and significant way. The cause was so right, so just, and he was so proud.

Dr. Bullock arranged our interview with Mr. Dunjee for about ten days later, and we agreed on a time to leave for Oklahoma City. When the appointed time came, Bullock arrived to find me sitting on the porch swing with my mother. Bullock and I barely talked on the trip. He wandered down (and all over) the highway, puffing away on that foul-smelling pipe. Somewhere along the way we stopped and got a cold drink. Getting back in the car, Bullock finally spoke. He said he thought I had an excellent chance of being selected.

Roscoe Dunjee's office was in the three-hundred block of Northeast Second Street in Oklahoma City. "Deep Deuce," it was called. That block was a bustling black business area. In that one block was a barbershop, a funeral home, two full-service restaurants, a dry cleaner, drugstore, shoe repair shop, tailor shop, and a dance hall. We reached the *Black Dispatch* office in midmorning. Mrs. Cora Price, Dunjee's secretary, was expecting us and led us immediately to his office.

He was alone. His office, functional and uncluttered with pictures or adornments, held a large wooden desk with a swivel chair, three metal file cabinets, a small sofa, and two straight-backed chairs. Newspapers, news journals, letters, and such carpeted every square inch of his desk.

Mr. Dunjee was easy to meet. Dr. Bullock introduced me as the young lady about whom he had called. Dunjee smiled in recognition. He remembered me as one of the Langston students he had met with earlier, the ones that were so upset about the red mud. We sat down and exchanged the usual small talk. Bullock handed Dunjee my transcripts. He examined them carefully and smiled. The doctor told Dunjee that my father was a minister; in fact, he was state bishop of the Churches of God in Christ of Oklahoma. Dunjee asked about my husband, and I told him about Warren, who was overseas in the military, but who stood ready to give his full support. Both men agreed it was good that my father and husband were insulated from economic pressure. They were also aware that being a minister's daughter would attract support from churches of all denominations.

Dunjee usually assumed a certain posture when he was in deep thought. He would lean his chair back, clasp his hands behind his head, and look toward the ceiling. In that posture he told me that the struggle would be long, expensive, and possibly bitter. Did I have the necessary courage and patience? Could I remain poised under duress and pressure? Was I available to make speaking appearances to help raise money to carry on the litigation?

Yes. Yes. Oh, yes.

The meeting lasted about forty-five minutes. The three of us and Iowa, Dunjee's overweight bulldog, then went down the block to Lyon's restaurant. Iowa took up a waiting position near the door while we had lunch. It was at this time that I learned for certain that Thurgood Marshall would be heavily involved in the effort to integrate higher education in Oklahoma.

For all of his silence on the way, Bullock had strongly presented me. On the return trip I plied him with questions about what he thought of my chances. Did he read anything in Dunjee's body language? What do you think he meant when he said . . . ? Bullock said we would simply have to wait and see. He then closed his mouth down on his pipe, blew a blast of smoke, and wandered across the road's center stripe.

I told no one about Bullock's recommendation or our trip to meet with Roscoe Dunjee. As Bullock said, nothing was final yet. There was constant talk and conjecture within the family but no hint or inference to neighbors and friends.

About a week after the interview, Bullock called. I was not at home, so he gave the message to Mother: I had been selected. When I walked in the door, Lemuel and Mother were all smiles as they gave me the good news. After a happy family celebration, I got on the phone to spread the word around the community. Persons who were active in the local chapter of the NAACP gave me their excited congratulations and encouragement. Some people apparently did not know of the planned litigation and wondered what all the celebration was about. The news would not reach the white community of Chickasha or people across the state until I made application in January. When I called Dr. Bullock to thank him for his support, he told me that he, Dunjee, and I would be going to the Norman campus in a few weeks.

The day to apply for admission to the law school in order to initiate the legal battle finally arrived. I did nothing to prepare for the trip to Norman. I knew I would not be accepted, so there was really nothing to prepare for except being rejected, and how do you prepare for that? While I expected to be rejected, I did not expect a hostile mob awaiting us or that officials would be insulting in any way. We were making a dignified request, and I expected that we would be received in a dignified way. I did not know how people would react in the town or around the state. I did not anticipate they would be happy about it, but I was not dealing with them that day.

The day, January 14, 1946, was a cold one. Bullock picked me up early that morning and we drove to Oklahoma City and directly to the *Black Dispatch* office. Dunjee was waiting; he reminded me again that my application would be refused. We got into his car and headed south on old U.S. 77. Dunjee was no better driver than Bullock. The editor's style was to plow down the center of the narrow, old two-lane highway. We entered the gate of the North Oval (Parrington Oval) at the university. Because he could not find a legal parking place, Dunjee parked illegally, and we walked the short distance to Evans Hall, the administration building, which housed the president's office.

Dunjee said, "Girlie, are you nervous?"

"Yes, a little anxious and apprehensive," I replied.

"Well, that's natural, but I imagine the students and officials at the university will be more nervous than you when they find out why we're here."

We laughed. Bullock offered that Dr. George L. Cross, president of the University of Oklahoma, probably was already a bit anxious, since Dunjee had called him Sunday to

DR. GEORGE LYNN CROSS, PRESIDENT
OF THE UNIVERSITY OF OKLAHOMA,
CA. 1946. PHOTO COURTESY WESTERN
HISTORY COLLECTIONS, UNIVERSITY OF
OKLAHOMA LIBRARY.

notify him that he would be down Monday morning on "a
business matter."

Anxious or not, President Cross was relaxed and cordial
as we entered his office. I took a seat directly across from
him; Bullock and Dunjee each sat to a side. Bullock did not
speak during the session. He simply sat there looking and listening intently. Mr. Dunjee introduced Dr. Bullock and me
and told the president that I was there to apply for admission
to the university law school. Cross looked at me, and I nodded. Dunjee explained that I was not only an honor student
from Langston University but the daughter of Bishop T. B.
Sipuel, a prominent minister in the Churches of God in
Christ.

"She desires to enter the school of law in the University of
Oklahoma and will commute daily from Oklahoma City,"
Dunjee closed. Neither he nor Cross nor anyone else in that
little room had to explain the commuting phrase; regardless
of what the university decided, I could not live in the town of
Norman.

Dunjee handed Cross a certified copy of my college transcript. It was in the name Ada Lois Sipuel, the name that I

would continue to use through every step to follow. Dunjee explained that I was the wife of Warren W. Fisher, whom I had married during my junior year at Langston University. The president examined the transcript and nodded.

As Dr. Cross passed the transcript around to his assistants, I discovered myself actually believing that I would be admitted. After all, who could find logical or constitutional reason to reject me? Still, I knew that I *would* be rejected, but the rejection would have nothing to do with me, only with my race and color.

Professor Royden Dangerfield, who was with Dr. Cross, said he thought that a decision should first be made concerning my scholastic qualifications. When he saw my Langston transcript, he said it appeared completely adequate. "I cannot see how any question can be raised respecting this young lady's scholastic qualifications," he concluded.

President Cross agreed with that opinion. "I believe, however, you should take this transcript to the dean of admissions and have him pass on it," said Dr. Cross.

The transcript was then taken to the dean of admissions, Roy Gittinger. Dangerfield left the room, returning after a short while to tell us that Dean Gittinger had told him that the transcript met every demand of the law school and the university.

"That brings me then to the decision that I must make," said President Cross.

Bullock, Dunjee, and the NAACP had not been the only ones who acted in the aftermath of the McAlester convention. Immediately afterward, the governing board of all state colleges and universities had met in a little-publicized emergency assembly. At it they had passed a resolution. Dr. Cross took it out of his desk drawer and read it to us before handing the short typewritten statement to Dunjee. It read:

> There was a discussion concerning the newspaper reports of the question of Negroes attending the University. Following this discussion, Regent William Wallace moved that the Board of Regents instruct the

President of the university to refuse to admit anyone of Negro blood as a student in the University for the reason that the laws of the State of Oklahoma prohibit the enrollment of such a student in the University.

The motion was unanimously adopted.

Utterly nonplussed, the editor suggested that if Dr. Cross was going to deny me the right that I sought to exercise, he should make an official statement in writing to that effect, directed specifically to me, giving the exact reason. This, we all knew, was a critical moment. In theory (if not in justice), Dr. Cross might have cited any number of reasons for rejecting my application. He might have said that it was because Langston was unaccredited. He might have given no reason at all. Either circumstance would deny the obvious and somewhat impede the legal strategy. It was the law that we wanted cited, for it was the law's racial basis that we rejected.

By his forthright response, Dr. Cross agreed that our request was right and fair. The slightest smile touched his lips as if to say, "I'll give you anything you need to get into court." He then dictated the following, which was typed on university letterhead and handed to me:

This will acknowledge receipt of your application for admission to the. Law School of the University of Oklahoma. . . .

. . . the Dean of Admissions has examined your transcript from Langston University and finds that you are scholastically qualified for admission to the Law School of the University of Oklahoma.

However, I must deny you admission to the University for the following reasons:

1. Title seventy, sections 452 to 464, inclusive, of the Oklahoma Statutes, 1941, prohibits colored students from attending the schools of Oklahoma, including the University of Oklahoma, and makes it a misdemeanor for school officials to admit colored students to white schools; to instruct classes com-

posed of mixed races; to attend classes composed of mixed races.

2. The Board of Regents has specifically instructed the president of this Oklahoma University to refuse admission to Negroes, giving as a basis of their decision, the Statutes of Oklahoma.

Mr. Dunjee smiled wryly as Dr. Cross read the carefully worded statement. He told Cross he was well aware of the statutory provision concerning segregation. "After all," he said, "I'm a black man; I've lived with discrimination all my life."

We shook hands all around before leaving Dr. Cross's office and emerged to the outer area to discover several photographers and members of a campus race-relations group waiting. Not surprised, Mr. Dunjee announced that a suit would be filed seeking to secure my admission to the school. He also thanked President Cross for dealing forthrightly with the issue involved, observing that his written acknowledgment that I was in all respects qualified save one provided a perfect case for litigation charging discrimination on the basis of that one exception: race.

There was a brief photo session followed by a quick and pleasant lunch with some members of the faculty, students, and townspeople. It was a sack lunch, since no sit-down establishment would serve us. We then headed back to the car, still sitting illegally on the North Oval. We were happy to see that in all the excitement no officer had ticketed it. We were not in trouble with the law—not yet, anyway.

IF IT PLEASE THE COURT . . .

Mr. Dunjee, Dr. Bullock, and I drove back to Dunjee's office. The trip back to Oklahoma City was just as adventurous as had been the trip down to Norman earlier in the day. Our car continued to take its share of the road out of the middle, but the conversation was decidedly more relaxed than on the way down. The interview with Dr. Cross and the other university officials had gone well. Most of all, we had that precious letter with its confession that my rejection was due to one thing and one thing only: my race. We had accomplished that phase, and things were exactly as we wanted them at that point. Watching him in this initial action, I knew that Dunjee was the man to lead the struggle. He was a wise man. He had demonstrated wisdom in his general demeanor and the way he had made the request to Cross to put the university's rejection in writing addressed to me. The encounter reinforced my thoughts of him as a sapient and shrewd leader. I had heard him speak, but the meeting with Dr. Cross was the first time I had watched him in action. I was impressed—very impressed. When we reached Dunjee's office, he suggested that we call New York City. It was time to tell Thurgood Marshall of the day's events.

Between the time that I had seen him at Lincoln School and that day a decade or so later, Marshall had become the nation's foremost civil rights attorney. My early life and educational experiences were similar to those of Marshall in that we both attended segregated elementary and secondary schools. He attended an all-black college, Lincoln University in Pennsylvania. State segregation laws precluded his attending law school at the University of Maryland, near his home in Baltimore, so young Marshall had to commute daily by train to Howard University in Washington, D.C.

DR. W. A. J. BULLOCK, ADA LOIS, AND ROSCOE DUNJEE AT THE TIME OF THE FIRST
ATTEMPT TO ENROLL AT THE UNIVERSITY OF OKLAHOMA

The dean and architect of the Howard program was
Charles Hamilton Houston, an honor graduate of Dartmouth
and Harvard Law School and a protégé of Professor Felix
Frankfurter (later a United States Supreme Court justice). It
was Dean Houston's mission to prepare a group of young
scholars as attorneys who would not only be skilled in law
but would also be familiar with methods of sociology, economics, history, and other liberal arts disciplines. They
would not only be lawyers but also social engineers, using
the law as an instrument for social justice.

Houston had earlier scored victories in several civil rights
cases, including one in Oklahoma. In Sapulpa an African
American defendant had been convicted of murder. Houston
argued his case before the United States Supreme Court, and
the decision in the Jess Hollins case invalidated the arbitrary
exclusion of blacks from jury service. Other early attacks on
discrimination in Oklahoma, such as *Lane v. Wilson* (1936)
and *Guinn v. Oklahoma* (1915), won the right of suffrage.
The cases demonstrated the will and efforts in Oklahoma to
fight for rights secured in the Constitution.

Thurgood Marshall was the most famous of Charles Houston's cadre of social engineers. In 1933 Marshall had become legal counsel for the National Association for the Advancement of Colored People. In 1936 he won a decision that forced Maryland to admit a black applicant. In 1941 Marshall was in Hugo, Oklahoma, a small community nestled in the southeastern part of the state known as "Little Dixie." He defended W. D. Lyons, a black man accused of murdering an entire white family. The case had been brought to the attention of the NAACP by Roscoe Dunjee.

The Lyons case exposed barbaric police practices. The prosecution's case rested largely upon a confession following several days' systematic beating by a representative of the Oklahoma governor's office. The authorities also took Lyons to the victims' home, lashed him to a chair, and pushed a pan of bones from the murdered bodies into his lap.

Marshall passionately argued Lyons's defense before a Choctaw County jury, no member of which had ever seen a black man in court before in any capacity except as a defendant. For that matter, neither had anyone else in the area. So astonishing was the sight that Hugo and other nearby towns dismissed their high schools in order for the students to attend what the authorities may have regarded as a circus. What the students received was a lesson in constitutional law and the rights of their fellow citizens—a lesson that they assuredly had not been receiving in their schools. More important to Marshall was the lesson that his appearance imparted to the black portion of the segregated courtroom: people who had been pushed around for years finally had in the NAACP an organization that would help them.

Lyons was convicted but given life imprisonment, a sentence that signaled the jury's doubts of his guilt, and Marshall appealed his case all the way up to the United States Supreme Court. Marshall lost there, and W. D. Lyons continued to serve his life term. A portion of the considerable expenses incurred was paid by a special defense fund established by John Worley, the mayor of my hometown. Worley was a white man whom Mother and her caucus had helped elect after the Argo tragedy. The fund's first one hundred dollars came directly from the mayor's pocket—perhaps payment in part for the debt owed Henry Argo's people.

On that day in January 1946, Dunjee called Marshall and told him we had completed step one at the University of Oklahoma. After the editor gave him the a run-through of the day's activities, I spoke with Marshall. I learned in that first conversation that my famous advocate was a warm and gregarious man. Marshall explained that attorney Amos T. Hall of Tulsa would serve as resident counsel for my case. Hall's first step would be to file a petition for a writ of mandamus, a court order directing a public official to take some action that he or she is legally obliged to perform. In this instance, the order would direct the university's regents and other officials to admit me at once to the school of law.

Of less national renown than Thurgood Marshall, Amos Hall was a lawyer of great experience. I had heard much of his legal talents and had met him once when he spoke at Langston. He was an elegant orator, a learned legal scholar, and a fierce advocate. I felt comfortable with his preparing the petition for the writ. Hall and Marshall would be assisted by Robert Ming, a professor of law at the University of Illinois, and James Nabritt, Charles Houston's successor as dean of Howard University's law school. I would thus be represented by some of the top legal talent in the United States.

Later that day, Dr. Bullock and I returned to Chickasha. He stopped at my home to join me in telling my family about the events of the day. The remainder of the community—and the state and nation—received the news the next day.

Pictures and reports of the big story filled that day's newspapers. Although many later editorials took stands against my effort, the initial news accounts were factual, unbiased, and noninflammatory. Radio news programs also carried accounts several times for two or three days.

The day the story broke Dunjee called me. "Well, Girlie, they really got the story out, didn't they?" he laughed in that jolly little high-pitched chuckle in which he always cloaked happy news. The early coverage validated his prediction that every newspaper in the state would give front-page notice to the story. Believing that all injustice should be spotlighted, Dunjee was delighted that the press—whether for good purposes or not—was doing just that. I knew that his own paper, the *Black Dispatch*, was going to keep that spotlight shining—intentionally and intensely.

For a while the folks in Chickasha greeted me mostly with stares. I also received local and long-distance calls from acquaintances. Most were positive. A few callers expressed concern that I would be exposed to strong hostility. Some white community leaders who were friendly with our family called or came by to remind us that the game could possibly get rough. Were we sure I should be exposed to probable overt danger?

I appreciated the neighbors and others who gave me support. The negatives I shrugged off. In the early days I perceived little open hostility. People seemed more curious than anything else. One of the few even moderately hostile events occurred a few days after the news broke, when I went to an optometrist in Chickasha to be fitted for glasses. The man recognized me from news pictures. He said he had attended school with "colored people," pointedly adding, "I'm not saying whether I liked it."

For once, I controlled my smart mouth. I told him that the black students with whom he attended school probably had not asked him whether he liked it, so neither would I. Otherwise, there was no change in my normal daily routine during the early weeks.

One reason for the early calm may have been that many people did not believe that I was serious about attending the white state university. Most white newspapers across the state apparently assumed that I was not serious. The real purpose of the *Sipuel* case and the NAACP, they reasoned, was only to pressure the legislature and state regents to provide better facilities at Langston University. Applying at the

University of Oklahoma, they supposed, would force the state to make improvements at Langston. It would remain separate, but it might get a little closer to being equal. Maybe they would even pave the streets.

Such surmising missed the point that Roscoe Dunjee kept making so eloquently as he wrote in the *Black Dispatch:* "There is only one place in Oklahoma where the state provides tax supported opportunity to secure a law degree and that spot [is] the University of Oklahoma. . . . This young black girl has the same right to effectively utilize [the state law school] as persons of any other race. It is this right we seek."

For our part, we had no illusions. The legal paperwork had to designate officials at the university—one was Dr. Cross—as defendants in the suit. This was purely legalistic. From the very beginning I realized that resistance was coming primarily from certain elected officials, the legislature, and the constitution and laws of the state of Oklahoma.

Oklahoma's only change to its original Jim Crow constitution and first laws had been to amplify and reenforce them. Anticipating just such a circumstance as I now represented, the legislature in 1935 had begun setting aside token sums of money to help pay the out-of-state tuition fees for black citizens who sought degrees not available to them at home. The 1941 assembly had amended the school laws to declare it a misdemeanor for any school administrator to admit African Americans to a state school, for any person to instruct classes composed of mixed races, even for any person to attend such classes. Otherwise free citizens who violated any of these laws were subject to fines that ranged up to five hundred dollars. Moreover, each day's commission of such "crimes" would be deemed a separate offense, punishable by a separate fine.

Most of the university officials whom my suit targeted as defendants were victims of these laws. All of us knew where the fault truly lay: ultimately, with political leaders. More accurately, it lay with people who pretended to lead—if only to lead astray. Fred McDuff, a minor candidate in 1946's gubernatorial race, was one. Attempting to capitalize on what he arrogantly and ignorantly supposed was major black opposition to the case, McDuff claimed that a majority of both whites and blacks preferred segregated schools. Claiming to speak on behalf of both, he proposed to compound Oklahoma's original sin of segregation with the creation of a second and predictably underfunded all-black four-year college, to be located somewhere near Muskogee. Only slightly better hope came from the more serious candidates, all of whom paid lip service to improving black education but bound their promises within the limits of separate schools.

Only their relative civility separated their stance from the stated position of William H. "Alfalfa Bill" Murray. A chief author of Oklahoma's original constitution and the Speaker of the House that had enacted the first segregation laws, Murray had provided the state with entertainment but precious little else during his own governorship in the 1930s. By the 1940s what had once been his eccentricities worsened to idiocies. He began spending what little money he had to publish such trash as *The Negro's Place in the Call of Race*. A vicious and ignorant little book, it referred to me as the "yellow gal" who threatened to reject "the All Wise Creator's Admonition, 'Everything after his kind'" in favor of "Atheism, Race Mixture, and [the] Communistic Party Line."

We knew that in the end it would make little difference who sat in Oklahoma's governor's chair. Even a sane, responsible Oklahoma governor could not improve Langston beyond what the legislature was willing to spend, and historically that had been very little indeed. No level of spending could ever erase the stain of inferiority that segregation stamped on the school. Neither the governor nor the legislature could remove that stain, any more than they could repeal all of the Jim Crow laws and reverse the state's constitution. Blacks had to look to the courts, not to the legislature or governor's office, to remove the racial barriers.

My great confidence in the United States Constitution

erased any doubt in my mind that we would win. I believed the Fourteenth Amendment's statement that no state may deny any person the right to "equal protection of the laws." Those five words meant what they said. Besides, Dunjee and Marshall never allowed me to doubt. My concern was not if but when. Sometime, somehow, I was going to begin law school at that university, and I was going to finish it as a lawyer. I was through with "separate but equal."

If we needed any reason to doubt the effect of Oklahoma's separate but equal education on its best African Americans, my family and I learned the lesson firsthand while waiting for the legal wheels to turn in my case. After passing up Dr. Bullock's offer that he be the plaintiff, Lemuel had applied for admission to Howard University's school of law. I may have been getting all the publicity, but we all knew that Lemuel was the "brain" in the family. He had graduated from Langston University with an outstanding transcript and academic honors. Howard, however, rejected his application because Langston was not accredited by the North Central Association of Colleges and Secondary Schools.

Thousands of dollars would be required to finance the long legal battle. In addition to filing fees and deposits, there were travel costs for the attorneys and expert witnesses who were to be called from all over the United States. Before the suit was ready to file, Dunjee began to solicit contributions from churches, NAACP chapters, and individuals. My father was one of the first to rally the troops. At a meeting of COGIC's Sunday School Convention Planning Committee in Oklahoma City in February, Daddy urged committee members to support the NAACP project and to encourage members of their local congregations to contribute also. He backed his words with a substantial contribution of his own, one of the first to my defense fund.

In March Dunjee and I began a series of personal appearances and mass meetings. We both would speak, and I gradually became more comfortable and effective in speechmaking. We did not have large corporate or foundation contributors. All of the money came in small donations from individuals or by way of local groups and NAACP chapters. The Snyder chapter was an early contributor, sending $10 that first month. The Lawton NAACP chapter donated $60.25. The community of Bristow sent $2.15. Accompanying that check was a letter from Mr. A. J. Montgomery listing contributors as follows: A. J. Montgomery $.50, Mrs. Jennie Murlhey $.25, Landmark Baptist Church $1.40. In the 1940s a $10 personal contribution was sizable. We received that amount from a convict serving a life sentence at the McAlester state penitentiary. His name was W. D. Lyons.

....

Marshall and Hall made numerous trips to Dunjee's Oklahoma City office to prepare for the upcoming lawsuit. It was at the initial strategy session that I first met with Thurgood Marshall personally. Hall, Dunjee, Jimmy Stewart (a state officer of the NAACP), and Marshall were seated in the room when I entered. I was a bit nervous about meeting the famous barrister. I spoke to everyone, and then Dunjee told Marshall, "This is the young lady." Thurgood immediately put me at ease by standing up, shaking my hand, and then giving me a big, friendly hug. We were strangers no more.

Six feet, two inches tall, he was just as handsome and just as charismatic as I had remembered him from my teenage days. What I learned about him was that he was a gifted raconteur, his stories a steady source of insight, inspiration, and humor. Because most of his legal practice was south of what he always called the "Smith and Wesson line," he had traveled thousands of miles through rural, racist areas in the south. He had encountered the Ku Klux Klan, the White Knights, and every variety of hate and racist groups. One day at lunch with Dunjee, Jimmy Stewart, and me, he related an incident from the 1930s in Tennessee when he and a friend outran an armed lynch mob by racing down dusty back roads one night. On another occasion he told us how wary and cautious he had to be with southern sheriffs and policemen. He recalled an occasion when he was arrested in a small town in Georgia for some minor, trumped-up traffic violation. A big-bellied cop took him to the jail and booked him. The officer asked if Marshall was hungry. He was. When instructed to go across the street to a small café for coffee and a sandwich, Thurgood declined. "No thank you, no way," he remembered saying. "I'm hungry, but you'll have to handcuff me and escort me to the restaurant. I don't want to be shot in the back on a charge of trying to escape."

Marshall brought that kind of experience, savvy, and stamina to Oklahoma when he took on the *Sipuel* case. He may not have anticipated howling mobs or bigoted law enforcement officers, but he did expect staunch segregationists ready to employ every evasion to avoid the issue. In the 1930s he had faced overt racism of the cold and deadly sort. In Oklahoma in the 1940s he would face covert racism, more cunning but no less formidable.

When I applied for admission to the law school, I knew it would entail a long struggle, and I was anxious to get the suit filed. I called Dunjee a couple of times, asking when the action would start. The answer both times was identical: "Patience." He reminded me that, as general counsel of the NAACP, Thurgood Marshall had a heavy schedule, and Amos Hall also had a large practice to carry on in Tulsa. "Patience, Girlie, patience."

Finally, the long-awaited day arrived. On Saturday, April 6, 1946, Hall, Dunjee, and I drove to the Cleveland County courthouse in Norman. This time we traveled in Hall's car to prevent Dunjee from driving. The courthouse was supposed to remain open on Saturdays until noon, and we arrived well in advance of that hour. We found, however, that the district judge, Ben Williams, was not in. The clerk recognized us as we entered and said the judge was at his home in Pauls Valley, about thirty miles away. She was very hospitable and offered to contact him.

When reached, Judge Williams talked briefly to attorney Hall and agreed to come to Norman immediately. He arrived quickly in very casual attire and explained his absence, saying that he had planned to take his two sons fishing. He was happy to postpone the fishing trip in order to allow the legal action to begin.

The judge and Hall went inside his chambers, and a few minutes later Hall reappeared and filed the petition with the clerk. When Hall asked how much money was required for the initial filing fee, she smiled and said, "As much as possible." She knew this would be a long, drawn-out battle with heavy court costs. Dunjee personally paid the filing fee, which would be reimbursed by the NAACP.

The four of us chatted amiably as we left the courthouse together—the judge to get on with his fishing; Hall, Dunjee, and I to begin a long and twisting legal process. Williams's cordiality notwithstanding, I felt certain he would deny the writ of mandamus. Still, we had now taken step two in the protracted battle.

The remainder of the day was uneventful. There were no reporters when we exited the courthouse. I returned home and told the family what had happened. The waiting period was over. Now the legal action was starting.

....

The hearing opened on a typically hot, sweltering Okla-homa summer day, July 9, 1946, promptly at 10:30. Cleveland County's modest limestone courthouse was still without air conditioning.

The hearing was to consider my petition for mandamus and the state's response. In careful, precise legal language, Hall and Marshall had stated my position: that my application to the University of Oklahoma "was arbitrarily and illegally rejected pursuant to a policy . . . of denying to qualified Negro applicants the equal protection of the laws solely on the grounds of her race and color." Noting that the university operated the only public-supported law school in the state and the only one that I was otherwise eligible to attend, my petition prayed the court for "a writ of mandamus requiring and compelling" the University of Oklahoma and the named defendants "to comply with their statutory duty and admit the plaintiff."

Assistant Attorney General Fred Hansen argued the state's case, with the assistance of Maurice Merrill. Dr. Merrill was one of the defendants named in the petition because he was the acting dean of the law school. Their response denied that my rejection had anything at all to do with the U.S. Constitution's equal-protection demands. Oklahoma had met that obligation, they asserted, by allotting funds to pay tuition and transportation expenses to attend an out-of-state school. Moreover, the state had its own constitution and statutes, which explicitly forbade interracial schools. Finally, they maintained that my failure to petition the Oklahoma State Board of Regents to provide me a legal education in accord with state laws rendered this court action fatally premature.

All the stilted language and legal posturing disguised a major strategic confrontation involving the meaning of the Fourteenth Amendment of the Constitution, and perhaps of America itself. Although the NAACP and its legal defense fund had never wavered from its ultimate end of taking Jim Crow out of the nation's schools, there had been significant controversies over the means to that end. One side wanted to hit segregation and hit it head-on whenever and wherever it appeared. Charles Houston, Thurgood Marshall, and Amos Hall had held out for a more gradual tactic but one equally fatal to Jim Crow. That was to attack the separate-but-equal doctrine where it obviously did not apply: in those circumstances in which African Americans were provided no education at all. This was most conspicuously the case with graduate and professional education.

At the time, seventeen states plus the District of Columbia either required or allowed for segregated public schools. All of those offered some form of higher education for blacks— however miserable and unequal it was—but none offered a full range of degrees at those Jim Crow colleges. Blacks who sought medical or legal degrees, for examples, from one of those state colleges were just plain out of luck. The most they had was a token appropriation that would ship them out of state and out of the authority's hair. They did not always have even that.

That circumstance led to the NAACP's strategic decision to seek systematic relief on the grounds that out-of-state tuition arrangements violated the Fourteenth Amendment, even if the *Plessy* case's separate-but-equal formula were granted. No, the NAACP did not recognize *Plessy* as lawful. In these circumstances, however, even *Plessy* was not being followed.

The reasoning was that states could not possibly follow that formula, even if they wanted to do so in good faith. Already among the nation's poorest commonwealths, most of the states involved could hardly fund black law schools, medical schools, dental schools, and graduate schools at all, much less ones that could pretend to equal their long-established, all-white counterparts. Let them try it, and Jim Crow would die of financial self-asphyxiation. Professional and graduate schools were expensive, especially in terms of faculties and libraries.

Reality dictated where the choice would be made. All the strategy in the world would amount to nothing without the proper plaintiff, a person who was undeniably eligible to enter professional school and unquestionably capable of succeeding there. In the nature of things, that most likely would be an African American who would seek legal training. Moreover, judges were graduates of law schools. Surely they would see through any attempt to hoodwink them by throwing up an instant law school and claiming it the equal of the ones they themselves had attended.

In pursuit of that strategy, Charles Houston had filed and won a suit in 1938 in the name of Lloyd Gaines. A Missouri native and graduate of that state's all-black Lincoln University, Gaines had made application to the state-funded law school at the University of Missouri. School authorities had denied his application, offering instead the familiar out-of-state tuition alternative. Houston had persuaded the Supreme Court that

that alternative did not release the state from its constitution-al responsibilities. The court ruled that the plan or promise of Missouri to build a law school in the future was not a satis-factory remedy. The plaintiff's right, it said, was a personal right to which he was currently entitled. Lloyd Gaines was entitled to admission to a law school supported by and con-tained in the state of Missouri. The decision was a milestone but ended with that announcement. Lloyd Gaines disap-peared before he could enter the school. His whereabouts were (and remain) unknown.

I was well aware of the mysterious end of the Lloyd Gaines decision. It did not deter me from my commitment to go forward with this legal action, to win the struggle, and to earn a law degree from the University of Oklahoma. That was why I was sitting in a steamy courtroom in Norman, Oklahoma, on a very hot day in July 1946. Warren was not yet home from the war zone. I went to Oklahoma City the day before the hearing, and Hall, Dunjee, and I rode to the Cleveland County courthouse together.

When I entered the courtroom, all whispers and conver-sation stopped and the room fell absolutely silent. I felt an atmosphere of curiosity. The courtroom was almost full. Most of the spectators were white, but I recognized some African Americans, including Jimmy Stewart and Malcolm Whitby, a part-time reporter for the *Black Dispatch*, among the early arrivals. There was no jury because there was no dispute of facts, only of law; thus the judge alone would decide the outcome. If he refused to issue the writ, we would have to appeal to a higher court. I am sure that if he had issued the writ the state would have appealed.

When Judge Williams entered, I remembered him from our earlier meeting in April. At that meeting I had thought he was a nice person—a nice person that probably would rule against me. When he entered the courtroom the day of the hearing, I had the same thought. Mr. Hall and I sat at one table in the front of the courtroom. Assistant Attorney General Hansen and Dr. Merrill sat at the other table.

Roscoe Dunjee, sitting in the audience, reported overhearing the following conversation from one farmer to another: "My, but that's a purty girl. I've been waiting for her to turn around, fer I seed her picture some times ago and I picked her out from the back of her head."

Amos Hall presented my case in oral argument. He stuck to his intended script: Oklahoma was denying me equal protection of the law because it provided legal training to white persons at Norman while I, because of my race, was required to go out of state. He cited *Gaines* to declare the out-of-state tuition plan irrelevant and not satisfying the equal-protection requirement of the Fourteenth Amendment. He also spoke of the financial cost of continuing segregation:

> The requirements of the Constitution cannot be set aside in the maintenance of separate schools. The right to an education is a personal one, the courts have declared; and if Ada Lois Sipuel is the only one out of the 200,000 Negroes of this state desirous of securing education in law the state is required to give her that regardless of how expensive this dual system of education is.

Hall's statement was clear, his reasoning sound. How could that district court uphold Oklahoma in refusing me admission to the school? The only argument was in their defining equality of treatment. Doesn't Oklahoma understand what *equal* means? Hall was so forceful and his arguments so logical that for a moment I dared to hope that the judge would grant the writ. In listening, I could see no alternative, no legal or moral ground to support a decision against me.

Representing Oklahoma, Dean Merrill claimed there were several legal (if not moral) grounds for refusing the mandamus. Recapitulating the state's written argument, he pointed to the state's segregationist constitution and statutes, ignoring the immoral racism on which those rested. He also emphasized that I had not exhausted legal and administrative procedure. Noting *Gaines*, Merrill argued that I first should have given official notice to the Oklahoma Regents for Higher Education that I desired to study law, and I should have requested that they provide a school of law at Langston. Only if the board officially refused my request would I have the right to apply to the University of Oklahoma and to seek judicial remedy if denied. Finally, the dean argued that the relief sought in this case—a writ of mandamus—was inappropriate. Although courts can order public officials to follow the law, they cannot direct them to violate it; and "separate but equal" was still the law in Oklahoma.

The court recessed late in the afternoon. We waited into the evening at the courthouse and speculated about the decision, no one offering or taking bets that we would win. Just after eight o'clock, Judge Williams reconvened the court and announced that he was denying the mandamus. The basis of his decision was that the function of mandamus was to enforce obedience to law, not disobedience. His decision made no judgment on Dr. Merrill's argument concerning the requirement of notice. Hall said he would file a motion for a new trial and appeal to the Oklahoma Supreme Court. Two days later, Hall filed the routine motion for retrial. Williams just as routinely denied it. We then prepared our next step: appeal.

....

I had come to expect that summer's court defeat, and my attorneys counseled me to accept it. It was just another step toward the final showdown, part of building the record for final appeal to the U.S. Supreme Court. I suppose that they were taking it like lawyers. I was philosophical. The suit was becoming my life. My life, too, had its victories as well as its defeats. In the months before and just after the district court hearing I experienced both, intensely and personally.

Recently, Warren had been writing increasingly impatient letters. The war was over. He had survived and he wanted to get home. I wanted him there too, and every morning I would rush out to check the day's newspaper listing of the troops that were arriving at New York City. Only once did I fail to look. That was the day that a friend called and said, "I know you're celebrating."

I said, "What? Why do you say that?"

"Warren has landed in New York. As soon as he can get his papers cleared, he'll be home."

I ran from house to house until I found a neighbor with a newspaper. It was true. My Warren was coming home. He had not even called or written. I knew him. Mr. Fisher had to be planning a grand surprise, probably waiting to call me when he was a few hours away from home, once the army processed his discharge at Fort Chaffee, Arkansas. Well, Mr. Fisher was not the only Fisher that could plan a grand surprise.

Sure enough, the phone rang a few days later.

"Lois?" a deep, familiar voice asked.

"Yes?" I answered, trying to control my racing heart.

"Lois!" he repeated.

"Yes?" I responded.

"Lois! It's me—Warren. Guess where I am?"

"I don't know," I said. "Fort Chaffee?"

A few hours later he was ringing our doorbell.

The next surprises were of an altogether different order. In May 1946 I returned to Chickasha from a speaking trip and was shocked with the news of the death of Dr. Bullock. The last time I saw him he was as active and determined as ever, puffing away on that old pipe of his. While I was away he underwent surgery and died shortly thereafter. He had been my physician and my friend. I felt a great loss.

For much of Chickasha he had played at least one of those roles, and the entire town—much of the white and nearly all of the black population—turned out for his funeral. It was held at the Colored Methodist Episcopal (CME) Church, which he had so devotedly supported through the years. Roscoe Dunjee spoke at the funeral. He rightly called Dr. Bullock "the first citizen of Chickasha." He might have added Grady County and much of southwest Oklahoma also. Dunjee closed with words that were a fitting testament to this quiet man who had made the best of circumstances beyond any of our choosing.

"Something of his dogged tenacity and unselfishness jutted out during his last moments," Dunjee told us. "We went . . . to the hospital following his operation to find him cheerful, and the moment after the usual salute of friends, the deceased immediately went into a discussion of the Ada Lois Sipuel case. His very soul and being was wrapped up in the struggle for human freedom and a better day for black folk in this world." Sitting with my mother in the pew that day, I prayed that God would bless that soul and crown its struggle with victory. Little did I realize that another and greater loss awaited my family and me.

It was a balmy fall morning, September 25, 1946. Daddy had gone to Oklahoma City the day before to prepare for a meeting with district superintendents. The telephone rang at about eleven o'clock. Someone was calling to tell us that Daddy had been stricken and we should come. Mother, Lemuel, Warren, and I drove over. En route we were all silent, lost in our own thoughts. Somehow, none of my thoughts included death. It never entered my mind. He was ill. The very worst it could be was a stroke.

Even when we arrived at the place where the meeting was convened and saw five or six ministers standing on the porch, I did not think of death. Daddy was such a vigorous seventy-year-old, always so busy, alert, and active. Then we entered the sitting room. He was stretched out on a divan, covered head to toe with a white sheet. Then we knew. Our strong, wonderful father was gone. At least he had not suffered long in leaving this life. It had been a sudden death by heart attack. The four of us clung together at that moment for strength and comfort. Helen flew home from school in Chicago, and the family continued to cling to each other for weeks and months. Funeral services were held in Oklahoma City at the state headquarters of the Churches of God in Christ and in Chickasha. Several out-of-state ministers and bishops attended one or both of the services. We buried Daddy beneath the red soil of Grady County, a long way from the rich, black land that had treated him and his people so poorly in Mississippi.

....

Life went on. After Warren came home he got a job as night engineer with the Domestic Egg Corporation. The company produced powdered eggs, and there was nothing that ex-serviceman Warren Fisher detested so much as powdered eggs. Still, we needed the money.

I also needed to continue to help raise money to keep the lawsuit going. Over the next months Dunjee and I covered much of the state, meandering all over its roads. We went to Tulsa, Cushing, Crescent, McAlester, Boley, Watonga, Clinton, El Reno, Kingfisher, Enid, Bartlesville, Elk City, Idabel, Duncan, Lawton, Ardmore, and other cities. In time, we developed a regular pattern, a kind of road show that we presented at black churches and community centers. Wherever two or three African Americans might gather, there we were also.

Other persons occasionally joined our cast and touring group. By 1947 the full ensemble included Dunjee, Dr. William Boyd of El Reno, Professor Melvin Tolson of Langston, Jimmy Stewart, and myself. Dr. Boyd was state treasurer of the NAACP, and Dr. Tolson was a professor of creative writing at Langston. Both Dunjee and Tolson were excellent orators, but Tolson had one special gift: he could keep us awake and entertained, no matter how late and how trying the trip. We often rode with Dr. Boyd, who had a new car and was a good, safe driver. Dr. Tolson expounded away on literature, politics, and just about every other imaginable subject. From time to time, Dunjee would interrupt with a joke. Almost always, the only humor was in his utter inability to tell a joke right. Even if his joke was a good one, he would ruin it by becoming so tickled he would flub the punch line.

While he roared with laughter, we would try to interrupt him by asking, "What was your last line again?"

Tolson was superb at telling jokes and relating anecdotes. He pantomimed, used dialect and accents, and acted out the details. Most of the jokes were nonethnic. Some, however, involved "these two Negroes," or began, "There was this Negro man and white man . . ." I noticed that if the jokes were nonethnic, you could never predict the outcome, but I saw a pattern in the black/white jokes: the African American always won against "Massah," "Mr. Charlie," or "The Man," the weapons of choice being innuendo, slyness, trickery, and cunning.

In November 1946 Chickasha hosted the annual NAACP state convention. It was the first time a large black convention had met in our small town. Most of the black community was involved in one way or another. A successful and well-ordered meeting would be a kind of memorial to Dr. Bullock. Townspeople also wanted to show that they were proud of and had confidence in the hometown girl. A tribute to Dr. Bullock and a discussion of the *Sipuel* case received top billing on the convention's agenda.

Two of Mother's friends, R. C. Alexander and Mrs. Wilhelmina Richie, were co-chairpersons of the convention. Mrs. Eva Boyd, my high school music instructor, directed the Lincoln School choir for entertainment. Citizens fed the delegates in various local churches. In the 1940s white-owned hotels and motels did not accept black travelers, and only in the larger cities such as Oklahoma City and Tulsa were black-owned facilities available. Chickasha had none. It was necessary, therefore, for residents to provide lodging in their homes for the delegates. My family kept two delegates.

Carloads of travelers came from all over the state. The memorial for Dr. Bullock occupied the afternoon of the first day. CME bishop J. M. Hamlet of Kansas City delivered the eulogy. Roscoe Dunjee also spoke about his long friendship with Bullock, recounting their experiences in fighting bigotry all the way back to Henry Argo's lynching in 1930.

I addressed the conference on Friday night at the grand finale, which was held in the Lincoln School auditorium. As I followed my familiar path to the school from our home only a couple of houses away, I reflected that much separated that night's visit from my first-grade experiences there. I talked of how long and how well my family had known Dr. Bullock. I told how it was he who had recommended me to become the "guinea pig" in the case. I told how we both shared a strong sense of justice. The University of Oklahoma project, I said, transcended a tribute to him and a challenge to me. It was also an opportunity for all of us to help make democracy a reality.

On this occasion, the "us" included white people from the university and its community. Thirty to forty people drove over from Norman to attend the convention. These included representatives of the Norman chapter of the Southern Conference of Human Welfare, the University of Oklahoma post of the American Veterans Committee, the campus chapters of the YMCA and YWCA, and the Westminster Group of the Presbyterian church, along with other interested Norman townspeople and university students.

Ben Blackstock, an OU student, addressed the convention. He was the brother of Robert Blackstock, a law student whom I had met as a member of the race relations group that shared lunch with us on the cold January day when all of this started. Ben said he spoke for many students: "We are solidly behind Miss Sipuel in her desire to enter school with us. We believe she will be a great asset to the university."

As welcome as was the goodwill of these individuals, none of us doubted that institutional forces were still arrayed against us. Blackstock himself addressed one such force. The University of Oklahoma, like other colleges and universities in the state, observed Religious Emphasis Week each year. Normally, the Oklahoma Memorial Union hosted all of the events. But the student union, although located at the heart of the campus, was independent of the university and was controlled by its own board of governors. That group absolutely forbade blacks entering the facility in any capacity except as servants and clean-up people.

In spring 1946 the committee in charge of the religious activities had invited a group of distinguished religious leaders from across the nation as participants. One invitee was the Reverend Hubert King, a black man who was chaplain of Teachers College, Columbia University. The union's governing board gave notice that if he entered the building, both he and every other participant would be criminally charged. The Religious Emphasis Committee faced a dilemma: either cancel the invitation to King or cancel the entire week's program. The group canceled the program, and the university had no Religious Emphasis Week for the first time in memory.

Some of us wondered what that said about the status of Christian charity during the other fifty-one weeks of the year. We all knew one thing: students had feelings; but governors, boards, and such had power.

....

In February 1947 Amos Hall told Dunjee and me that the Oklahoma Supreme Court had scheduled a hearing on our case for the morning of March 4. He also had one other piece of news: He and Thurgood Marshall would share the oral argument before the court. I was thrilled. My problem was to keep my excitement contained. It was like waiting for Christmas. I spent the time marking the days off the calendar.

With the countdown nearly at zero, I came to Oklahoma City the day before the hearing. The morning of the hearing, Dunjee picked me up and drove me to the state capitol. I had never been inside the capitol before.

Happily, there were no spectators or reporters outside or in the corridors. Dunjee and I made our way to the fourth-floor courtroom. When we entered the marble and oak-paneled chamber, Hall and Marshall were already there, seated at one of the long tables. Seated at the other long table were Dr. Merrill and Assistant Attorney General Hansen, both once more representing the state. The room was not yet full, but by the time the proceeding began there was standing room only.

The written pleading of each side was essentially the same as in the Cleveland County District Court. During oral arguments, the attorneys advanced their respective positions, the give-and-take sharpened by probing questions from one or more of the nine justices. Most questions came from one judge, Associate Justice Earl Welch. For example, when Amos Hall maintained that Oklahoma's action violated equal protection of the law, Justice Welch interrupted.

If the state was guilty of this in 1947, he asked, was it also guilty in 1908, when it enacted the original laws? I was not yet an attorney, but I instantly knew what my answer was. It was yes, the state was wrong in 1908 and every year since. It may have been legal, but it was still wrong. After the *Gaines* decision of 1938, it was both wrong and illegal.

Welch persisted by inquiring, "Is it your contention that when a law school was set up at the University of Oklahoma, an equal school should have been set up for Negroes?" Hall answered, "Perhaps it would be expensive to establish a school offering equal opportunities to our people, but separation is a condition established by the state and one for which we did not ask."

During the state's portion of the argument, Hansen emphasized the technical point that I had not given state authorities prior notice of my desire for legal training before filing the suit. He also went out of his way to tell the court that the NAACP brief was prepared in New York City, and he implied that Marshall was an "outside troublemaker." He said that the intent of the "New York" brief was to break down segregation. He said that attorney Hall did not concur in that idea.

Hall quickly said that he was indeed opposed to segregation in all areas. In this case, in this court, on this day, however, the issue was something different: Was the state denying or providing this plaintiff's constitutional right to equal protection of its laws? Marshall further refuted

Hansen's statement concerning the "New York" brief, inform-
ing the court that the brief was researched and prepared by
Mr. Hall in Tulsa, aided and assisted by several NAACP
lawyers. It was printed in New York for convenience and
expediency. He also ignored that diversion to return to the
real issue, closing his argument with the question "Does the
Constitution apply now, or will we have to wait?"

We had the right answers, but the state was not even asking the right questions. As we left the courtroom, Dunjee
detected a bit of frustration in my attitude. "Chin up, Girlie,"
he said. "I agree with your expectation that the decision will
not be in our favor, but that will not be the final word."
Marshall gave me a friendly hug and wink. He said this hearing was a necessary part of the procedure. "Now we're really
on our way."

After the hearing I reflected on the arguments and the attitude of the assistant attorney general and the state justices. I
still believed that the overriding question involved
Oklahoma's concept of fairness and integrity. Even if fairness
were set aside, even if the federal Constitution did not exist,
Oklahoma's own laws mandated equality of educational
opportunity and facilities. Did the people of the state and
their elected officials honestly believe that Oklahoma had
obeyed that law?

My answer came about six weeks later. On April 29 the
Oklahoma Supreme Court issued its opinion and affirmed the
decision of the district court. I first heard it on the radio.
Dunjee called me soon afterward and said that the decision
was as we expected. The Oklahoma Supreme Court had
upheld the state's statutory and constitutional provisions
requiring separate schools. Acknowledging *Gaines*, however,
the court ruled that the equal-protection clause of the United
States Constitution required that equal facilities must be provided within the state. Again pointing to *Gaines*, the court
insisted on a precondition, that notice be given of the resident's desire for training in a specific area.

Some persons saw the decision as one that afforded the

state an opportunity to negotiate with the NAACP and black educators concerning the upgrading of Langston or the possibility of joining with other states to establish regional professional and graduate schools. The NAACP and I would have nothing to do with that. One way or the other, we wanted the barriers down, not lowered or moved.

Even had we been willing to accept a compromise, no one offered us one. NAACP attorneys had requested an opinion as early as possible. The Twenty-second Legislature was then in session, and the case gave policy makers, including the legislators, regents, and Governor Roy J. Turner, plenty of time to act. While the court had deliberated, the governor, legislature, and boards of regents did nothing. Although two and a half weeks remained in the legislative session after the court rendered its judgment, all remained equally inactive. After the session ended, they would not return to the capitol for two years. I knew that if it were up to them and other state officials, I would be seeing freeze warnings for hell before I found justice at their hands.

My attorneys and Dunjee had prepared me well. I had not really expected the state supreme court to reverse the district court's ruling, but I have to admit that until that very moment I had still hoped. The adverse decision meant a long journey to the Supreme Court of the United States and many months of additional litigation and waiting.

I confronted that prospect knowing that a gross injustice was being done. I was more determined than ever to continue with the litigation—one year, or two years, or however long would prove necessary. Oklahoma had shown me that I was not going to get justice in its courts or within its borders. For the first time in the entire process, I was angry.

My attorneys routinely applied to the state court for a hearing. The court routinely refused. We then petitioned the United States Supreme Court for a writ of certiorari early in Fall 1947. This is an order from a high court to a lower court directing that records in a particular case be forwarded to the high court for review. It is discretionary with the high court, and many more applications for the writ are denied than are granted. If granted, it gives the high court the opportunity to review the case. It does not signal that the review will end in a reversal of the original judgment, merely that a significant constitutional issue is involved that the court wants to examine.

Marshall and Hall directed their petition to just that issue. At the time, *Gaines* was still the governing law on school cases, and the two attorneys maintained that Oklahoma had flagrantly violated that ruling. *Gaines* had granted Missouri and other states the right to maintain separate but equal professional schools but only under certain circumstances. *Sipuel v. Board of Regents of the University of Oklahoma* compelled the Court to define those circumstances precisely. When no separate (let alone equal) facility existed for African Americans, ought not a state be compelled to admit black citizens at once to its previously all-white institutions? My attorneys answered yes.

More important than that answer, however, was the answer to another question. Surprisingly, it was the first time that the NAACP had directly laid that question before the Supreme Court. As the *Sipuel* brief put it, "Beyond that the petitioner contends that the separate but equal doctrine is basicly [sic] unsound and unrealistic and in the light of the history of its application should now be repudiated."

There it was. Forget the legal mumbo jumbo about out-of-state tuition grants, prior notification, administrative relief, and all the rest. We were measuring Jim Crow's neck for the executioner's noose. Deliberate and farsighted strategists, brilliant and impassioned litigators, obstinate and insensitive state policy makers, and a very angry plaintiff had come together in one place at one time to confront the nation's highest tribunal with a lawsuit that tested the meaning of our nation's Constitution and the quality of its conscience.

When Thurgood Marshall called me to say that the Court had granted our petition, I was thrilled. When he asked if I would like to attend the hearing, my one-word answer—

"Yes"—contained all of the anger and frustration and hope that I could summon.

....

Even before the Supreme Court heard my case, it was having its effect. For one thing, Howard University made special arrangement to admit Lemuel to its law school. I would be staying with him in Washington while he completed his second year of law school as I awaited the Supreme Court decision to let me begin my first.

News that the Court would review my case also stiffened the resolve of NAACP members back in Oklahoma. The state organization held its annual convention in Idabel just after the Court granted the petition, and the *Sipuel* case received considerable attention from Roy Wilkins and other national officers who spoke there. One piece of bad news partially offset the enthusiasm, however.

About a week before the convention, Roscoe Dunjee had called me to his office. As I entered he looked at me rather intently, and I sensed that something important was weighing heavily on his mind. Assuming his familiar pose of leaning backward with his eyes cast toward the ceiling, he said, "Girlie, I'm going to resign as state president of the NAACP for health reasons."

"Oh, no, Mr. Dunjee," I said, "we need you."

"I'm not going anywhere. I'll be right here," he said, "but my doctor and I agree I must limit my travel and activity." I sat down and twisted a pencil nervously. I did not want him to resign, yet I knew he was advanced in age, and he had served the organization and the entire cause of human rights for many years. If he needed to lighten his load, then he should do so. Like he said, he still would be there with advice and guidance.

Dunjee did not attend the thirteenth annual convention, at which his resignation was announced. It was better that he was not present; emotions were too strong. Jimmy Stewart read the president's annual message, which reviewed past achievements of the organization. The statement then explained that reasons of health dictated his decision to resign as the organization's leader. At first there was shocked silence, then murmurs of surprise, and finally tears. The conference adopted a resolution regretfully accepting the resignation and thanking him for his years of courageous leadership.

Dunjee could not accompany me to Washington, and neither could Warren. Warren had left his temporary job in Chickasha and taken a job in his brother's machine factory in Providence, Rhode Island. We were there when Marshall told me of the Supreme Court's order for certiorari. Warren would stay there doing his job while I went to Washington to do mine.

One comfort of our stay in Rhode Island was that it removed me for a short time from what Mother referred to as "ugliness." As my case progressed and the issues became more tightly drawn, I had begun to receive many letters from cities and towns in Oklahoma and from other states as well. Some letters were from people I knew, and others were from total strangers. There were good letters and bad ones. Some used abusive language to tell me that I should learn to stay in my place. One called me a "stringy-haired, tall, skinny, sallow-faced negress" who was only a few generations from the jungles of Africa. A few threatened physical violence if I returned to the University of Oklahoma campus. One letter was addressed simply to "Ada Lois Sipuel, nigger, Oklahoma." It came directly to my home.

I tried to shrug off such letters as the actions of ignorant, small-minded people who did not have the courage to identify themselves. Generally they made me angry and a bit frustrated. They made my mother furious. As fast as she read them, she destroyed them. I suggested that we keep them for souvenirs, but she refused to have such ugliness around.

I have no idea what the proportion of that ugliness was to the total, but the letters did express one current of public opinion. More representative were the letters to the editors carried in the OU campus newspaper, the *Oklahoma Daily.* The paper had asked its readers, "Do you think that Miss Sipuel should be allowed to enroll in law school at the University of Oklahoma in view of the fact that Langston does not offer work in this field?" Most supported the admission of African Americans. Those that were opposed did so because of the racial mores of that period. Fairly typical were the following responses:

- Dick Holbert, a sophomore in business administration: "The state should maintain a law school at Langston. I'm not a proponent of racial superiority, but I do insist on racial segregation."

- Charles Smith, a University College freshman: "Definitely think she should. She's entitled to an education too."

- Bob Shockley, an engineering student: "I don't know whether I want 'em around or not."

- H. L. Kelley, a junior in engineering: "She should be admitted here or prepare Langston so she can study law there."

One particular comment drew considerable attention. Wayne Biddle, whom the *Daily* identified as a junior majoring in petroleum engineering, was quoted as saying, "I don't think so. In the event she is allowed to enroll, she wouldn't be allowed to stay because she won't be able to maintain an acceptable grade average."

Among those who responded to Biddle was Nadene Hahn, who said that his letter was "just plain stupid." She challenged him to compare his grade average with mine, adding that African Americans had more obstacles to overcome to obtain an education than did whites.

Mr. Biddle refused to alter his position, however:

Editor of the *Daily:*

"Yah suh boss, ah won the case in the Supreme Court, and ah am ready to enter law school."

> Yes, Miss Sipuel, you won a case in equity but you have yet to win the most important challenge—personalities. . . . Rigid control is the only solution to a problem of this type. Entrance of one Negro in one school will pave the way for those awaiting the decision of this case.
>
> WAYNE BIDDLE

Through the fall semester the debate continued. By late November Quinton Peters, the student editor of the paper, offered his own opinion in a speech delivered on WKY radio and printed in the *Black Dispatch*. Acknowledging that opinions were pretty much on the side of admitting me, he pointed out that the letters did not necessarily represent the opinion of the majority of students on campus, only the opinions of those students who had taken time to sit down and write a letter to the editor. As for himself:

> It is a known fact that any Oklahoman who advocates this business of giving the state Negroes a professional education is going to be branded a . . . may I use the term? . . . lover, "Negro lover." Yet in 1947, in Oklahoma, that's the status of the problem.
>
> I don't know a Negro personally. I have worked with Negroes . . . and have had my share of trouble with them. . . . But, I feel that the very things that make the Oklahoma Negro the problem he is today could be vastly improved if he were educated.
>
> How can we whites expect the poor devil to practice cleanliness if he doesn't know the evils and loathsomeness of dirt? . . . How can we expect him not to have a shack full of hungry kids he can't support when he doesn't even know the way the white man goes about in keeping their children down to the supportable minimum?
>
> There is no alternative. You have to educate him. You don't have to marry him.

If the editor believed his opinion a moderate one, there were many prepared to disabuse him of that notion.

Because of the widespread coverage of his remarks, Peters was one of thirteen students from the University of Oklahoma invited to attend a student conference at Langston University in December. The *Oklahoma Daily* described the students who attended as "curious." None of the four who had previously identified themselves as opposing admission of African Americans to the all-white university experienced a change of heart. Although they met with President Harrison, the only complimentary report the group made was of the dinner they were cooked and served by Langston's students. They did not even notice that there still was just one fully paved street on the Langston campus. A thunderstorm struck while the visitors were there, but it was the meal and the service, not the mud and the injustice, that impressed them.

So the students returned to their all-white campus in their all-white town. I headed for Washington, where the United States Supreme Court sat in a building that proclaimed the Court's purpose and my expectation. "Equal Justice under Law," it said on the outside. I expected that it would say the same on the inside too.

. . . AND OTHERS SIMILARLY SITUATED

My case was set for argument on January 8, 1948. It was nearly two years to the day since Dr. Bullock, Mr. Dunjee, and I started down Highway 77 to the registrar's office at the University of Oklahoma. On this January day, unlike that one, I was confident of success. After so many long delays, the high court had scheduled the hearing for the first available date. If the Constitution meant anything, it had to mean that I was going to be starting law school—in the second semester, which would begin on January 29. Why else did the Court respond to my petition for certiorari so swiftly?

It was a cold day, but one of crystalline purity. There I was, a preacher's daughter from little Chickasha, Oklahoma, climbing the steps of the United States Supreme Court building. My eyes caught the words "Equal Justice under Law." Amos Hall, Thurgood Marshall, and I entered the building ahead of schedule. We walked down the wide corridor, its way marked with uniformed military personnel standing at attention at spaced intervals. Finally we came to the Court's chamber. The awesome sight seemed a fitting end of a journey two years in the making.

The chamber had plush carpet and carved, heavily padded pews for spectators. The Court's sergeant-at-arms sat in a high chair facing the audience. Behind him was the judge's bar, beautifully carved and long enough to accommodate nine large, overstuffed leather chairs, one for each of the nine justices. Behind the chairs was a heavy velvet curtain. The bailiff announced the imminent appearance of the justices, and everyone stood. The judges then stepped through the nine slits in the curtain.

I was thrilled. I recognized a few of them from photos that I had seen. The real thrill came from my sense that this august body was assembled that morning because of me—to recognize and affirm my rights of citizenship.

The briefs of both parties repeated most of the points raised in earlier hearings. My brief repeated the position that the separate-but-equal doctrine was not applicable in those circumstances in which a state provided neither separation nor equality. This time, however, it added the powerful issue that the doctrine itself was invalid and asked the Court to end it. If all went well, that would define the structure of the two-hour oral argument. Each side was given one hour to state its case and argue its merits.

As had been true at the state supreme court, the judges were free to interrupt counsel for either side at any point. This time, however, it was the state's counsel that was being interrupted. Marshall carefully presented his argument with scarcely an interruption. I believed that only one decision was plausible: my immediate admission to the University of Oklahoma. That seemed the only way Oklahoma could comply with the United States Constitution.

Attorneys Hansen and Merrill had a much harder and slower go of it. The state attorneys reiterated their position concerning out-of-state tuition and my failure to give the board of regents notice of my desire to study law within the state. They also spoke of the Oklahoma law prohibiting whites and blacks from attending classes together. Various justices cut in on the arguments with rather pointed questions that seemed to indicate they were leaning in my direction. At least as important as the questions' wording was their tone, a tone that ran all the way from incredulity to frustration with Oklahoma's position.

Justice William O. Douglas cut in on Merrill's and Hansen's point about the lack of prior notification to observe that I had attempted to enroll on January 14, 1946, and filed suit almost two years ago. Douglas opined that that would appear to be clear notice. He said that at the rate the state was moving I would be an old lady before I would be able to practice law. Justice Robert Jackson wanted to know why, after two years, Oklahoma had made no effort to do anything about the problem. Justice Hugo Black also specifically wanted to know whether the regents had taken any action to satisfy my effort. Hansen had no direct response, saying only that the regents had no money to set up any other law school, adding that they believed I would refuse to accept a segregated law school.

Justice Felix Frankfurter systematically explored various alternatives and asked whether the state would admit me for the term beginning in a few days if the Court mandated it to do so. Hansen answered yes, if necessary, although he added that doing so would violate the laws of Oklahoma. Frankfurter then asked if a separate course of study could be arranged within the existing law school. Hansen answered that it could. Could I be admitted temporarily pending the establishment of a separate law school? Hansen said that the Oklahoma Board of Regents for Higher Education had authority to do any or all of those things.

Justice Robert Jackson interrupted to ask if counsel really believed that a school with a single student could afford an acceptable legal education. Merrill answered yes. Justice Jackson disagreed. He said such foolishness was neither reasonable nor equitable.

Dean Merrill noted that Oklahoma was one of many states with a public policy of segregation. He reminded the Court that for decades rulings had upheld that arrangement. Now, he told the Court, plaintiff is unwilling to recognize that settled policy. He was right on that.

Justice Jackson asked why I should be required to abide by a given policy more than any other person. Should I, he asked, be required to waive my constitutional rights for the benefit of the state's public policy?

They were good questions—great questions, it seemed to me. They were exactly the questions that every other court and public official had ignored. This time, this Court asked them.

Only four days after the hearing, the Court issued a terse

one-page, unsigned unanimous order. With OU's second semester's enrollment to begin in exactly one week, the judgment was that I was "entitled to secure legal education afforded by a state institution." The Court ordered that Oklahoma "provide it for her in conformity with the equal protection clause of the Fourteenth Amendment and provide it as soon as it does for applicants of any other group." It issued a mandate that reversed the judgment of the Oklahoma Supreme Court and remanded the case to that court for proceedings not inconsistent with the United States Supreme Court.

Dunjee was the first to phone me in New England with the news. He was jubilant and so was I. It was as if Christmas, New Year, and the Fourth of July were all wrapped in one large, beautiful package. Marshall called me next. He, however, was more restrained. He said it could possibly be the victorious end to the long legal battle. He had fought enough battles to know that the battle was not over until I was enrolled in the law school. He told me to return to Oklahoma immediately and prepare to seek enrollment.

Newspapers across the nation carried the story. Dunjee's *Black Dispatch* reported the news with unconcealed glee, declaring that the state would have to admit me to the university immediately. The *New York Times* seemed to agree, pronouncing the decision "a move of startling suddenness." The *Washington Post* quoted Oklahoma's chancellor of higher education, Dr. M. A. Nash, as saying that the state would of course obey the ruling. One day after the Court's decision, Oklahoma City's *Daily Oklahoman* published the results of what it claimed was a scientific poll of student attitude at the university. A tiny percentage—5 or 6 percent—wanted to continue to resist my admission outright, but fully 82 percent of the law students said that they were ready to welcome me to their classes.

It seemed to me that things were just about as good as they could be. I would take 82 percent any day. What I did not notice, however, was that the news reports were all conspi-

LEAVING WARREN, AND RHODE ISLAND,
AFTER THE SUPREME COURT'S FAVORABLE DECISION

cuously silent regarding the responses of the state's public officials. Both Governor Turner and the university officials refused to comment. About the only one who did so was Mac Q. Williamson, the state's attorney general, its chief legal officer, and Fred Hansen's superior. Williamson was one of the few to note in all of the excitement that the Court's short and plain order had not specifically stricken down Oklahoma's segregation laws. Williamson had a congenital inability to pronounce the word Negro. He always said "nigra," and I regarded his legal acumen to be no greater than his language skills or his moral sensitivity. I prepared to go home to Oklahoma and to go to school.

I left Rhode Island and Warren on January 14, 1948. There was sleet and a snow blizzard. Planes were running late, but I was finally on my way. When the plane landed at the Oklahoma City airport that Wednesday evening, persons on the side facing the terminal looked out their windows and wondered what was going on. Who on the plane was attracting the spectators, flowers, and newspaper reporters? they

ADA LOIS WITH
HER MOTHER AT THE
OKLAHOMA CITY
AIRPORT, READY TO
ENROLL AT THE
UNIVERSITY OF
OKLAHOMA

asked among themselves. I knew, but no one asked me. When I stepped out of the plane, I waved happily. Mother was the first person to embrace me. Dunjee was close behind and whispered to me to be careful in answering questions of reporters. Yes, I had thought we were going to win. When would I be enrolling? Just as soon as possible. "It's a wonderful Constitution," I ended. "I'm going to become a lawyer." Dunjee's whispered caution and the look on his face told me that something was not quite right.

Dunjee escorted Mother and me to his car and drove us to the home of a friend, Mrs. J. V. Hearne. A meeting with NAACP officials had been planned to convene immediately upon my arrival. At the meeting, Dunjee said the *Sipuel* decision was not as definitive as we had hoped. It appeared that Oklahoma might try to evade the Supreme Court by setting up a sham law school somewhere. We would just have to wait for the state court to write its order interpreting the decision.

I kept my silence—just as Oklahoma's public officials kept theirs. No state official wanted the responsibility of saying that I should be allowed to enter the University of Oklahoma. At the same time, none of them wanted to defy openly the United States Supreme Court. The state supreme court held several conferences concerning the decision between Wed-nesday and Friday. It issued its opinion on Saturday, January 17, at 3:00 P.M. The order directed the Board of Regents for Higher Education either to close the law school for white students or to afford me and others similarly situated educational opportunity in accordance with the Fourteenth Amendment of the United States Constitution. Either way, it insisted that the state preserve the segregation requirements of Article 13 of the Oklahoma Constitution and 70 Oklahoma Statutes, sections 451–57. The order further directed the trial court in Cleveland County to take such proceedings as necessary to carry out these orders. Again, it demanded that those proceedings must preserve Oklahoma's separate-but-equal system.

Oklahoma was not giving in. Reporters called my home, but I was out of town, hurriedly trying to raise more money for the next round's legal contest. They asked my mother's thoughts about developments in the case. She told them, "I don't think they can set up equal facilities someplace else, but I don't want to speak for my daughter." She was right. Dr. H. W. Williamston of Idabel, president of the Oklahoma NAACP, was just as right when he told the reporters, "It is our belief that there can be no equality in segregation." He added, "If it should appear that the order of the Supreme Court is not being followed we would resume the legal fight." About the only thing Dr. Williamston got wrong was his declaration that "the state of Oklahoma is too honorable to try to circumvent the ruling of the United States."

Honorable or not, the state's response came with a speed that demonstrated unabashed and unashamed determination.

Attorney General Williamson issued a resolution ordering the state board of regents to establish a Langston University College of Law, to be located in the state capitol and fully operational by the following Monday, January 26, 1948. By prearrangement, James C. Nance, president pro tem of the senate, announced that several fourth-floor committee rooms would be turned over to the new school. The state law library on the first floor would serve as the separate law school library.

The chairman of the state regents, R. T. Stewart, made the public announcement of the separate law school as a division of Langston University on January 24, two days before the school would open. After a conference between the president of Langston and the Oklahoma Regents for Higher Education, Stewart emerged to claim that the state was making a bona fide effort to provide adequate facilities. Frank Buttram, an Oklahoma City oil millionaire and a major force among the regents, announced the faculty appointments. Jerome E. Hemry, a practicing lawyer of twenty years' experience, was named dean at a salary of six thousand dollars a year. Randell S. Cobb, a former state attorney general, was named professor at a salary of five thousand dollars, and Arthur Ellsworth was appointed professor at a salary of forty-five hundred dollars a year. The positions were obviously part-time jobs, but Buttram announced that the three were ready to devote the full time required to conduct the law school and afford any student entering full opportunity. Each instructor would continue his private practice.

Pointing to the quality of the faculty and the existence of the state law library, Buttram pronounced that in such aspects the Langston law school was every bit equal—even superior—to that at the University of Oklahoma. Regent Buttram insisted that "We are serious when we say . . . we have set up an equal [school with] . . . even better facilities than the average student at the University of Oklahoma [is provided]." Regent John Rogers chimed in with the declaration that "a student can probably learn more at the new school than at Norman." A prominent Tulsa attorney, Rogers said he would have no reluctance to appear before the United States Supreme Court to argue for the substantial equality of the new law school.

Perhaps the most remarkable quality of all of these solemn announcements is that each of them was made with a straight face. There followed a telegram from Langston's president, Dr. Harrison, to me at my home in Chickasha, with a second copy sent to the home of Mrs. Hearne in Oklahoma City, where I stayed when in the capital. Registered letters to confirm the telegrams also went to both addresses. Over the signature of Dr. Harrison, Langston's president, these informed me that the Langston University law school would be operational and that registration would begin at 8:00 A.M. on Monday, January 26, in Room 426 at the State Capitol. Stewart said, "We are taking every precaution to be sure she is notified."

Oklahoma was not the only one that was not giving in. On the advice of Dunjee and Marshall, I went through the motions of reapplying to the University of Oklahoma's law school. The new dean of admissions, J. E. Fellows, went through the motions too. He had me fill out a new application, looked it over, and requested that I provide a certified copy of my freshman year's transcript from Arkansas A & M. I immediately contacted Pine Bluff and had an official copy of the transcript sent to the University of Oklahoma's office of admissions and records. I knew this was an exercise in futility. The Oklahoma courts and public officials had made it abundantly clear that the fight was not over. It would be won or lost in the courtroom, not in the admissions office. All that this step accomplished was to begin the painful rebuilding of the record.

With more court action ahead, Dunjee called on his friend the Reverend E. W. Perry, pastor of Oklahoma City's Tabernacle Church, for an emergency fund-raiser. By Saturday afternoon handbills circulated throughout Oklahoma City's black east side. That night approximately seven hundred people turned out for the mass meeting at Tabernacle. I made only token remarks because of a severe cold and sore throat. I thanked the audience for its support in what would not end until we had revolutionized educational opportunities for African Americans throughout the south. I talked of how Oklahoma officials had deprived me of what the U.S. Supreme Court had said was my constitutional right. I told the audience that my brother was discharged from the army about the time I first attempted to enroll at the University of Oklahoma in January 1946. My brother proceeded to enroll in the Howard University law school without any financial support from the state. He was then completing his second year, and I had yet to get enrolled. Reverend Perry kicked off the fund-raising with a fifty-dollar contribution and challenged all present to do their best. A total of seven hundred dollars in cash and three hundred dollars in pledges was collected. It was the largest sum raised in a single meeting during the entire legal controversy.

Amos Hall again appeared in the Cleveland County District Court seeking an order for my immediate admission to the University of Oklahoma. The judge was now Justin Hinshaw. Hall's position was that Judge Hinshaw should order my immediate admission to the University of Oklahoma because the newly created separate school was not equal and, for that reason, did not conform to the United States Supreme Court's ruling. Hinshaw ruled that there was no testimony or other evidence before the court concerning the quality of the new school; therefore, he was rejecting Hall's request. He issued an order that said, in effect, that the mere existence of a separate school was enough to prevent my immediate admission to the University of Oklahoma. Hall took exception to the order and gave notice that the order would be appealed.

I received the news on Sunday, January 25, one day before I had been instructed to report for enrollment at the fake law school. My attorneys would prepare the appropriate legal response. One thing was certain, though: I would not set foot in the new law school. State officials might have claimed the wondrous capacity to create in less than five days a school they claimed to be equal to the school at the University of Oklahoma, then nearly five decades old. They were not going to convince me of that. And they were not going to convince me to give up, either.

On Monday, January 26, I got dressed and went to apply—at the University of Oklahoma. To no one's surprise (including my own) the University of Oklahoma again refused me. Dr. Cross rejected my application through no wish of his own. The regents had ordered him to do so because they claimed that the instant school in the capitol was "substantially equal to the University of Oklahoma law school."

To no one's surprise (especially my own) not many other people were so persuaded either. That Monday the dean and faculty of the Jim Crow law school reported to the capitol. I did not go. Neither did anyone else. The faculty waited patiently until Friday, January 28, when the regular enrollment period ended at 5:00 P.M. Showing a brave face, Dean Hemry then announced that the faculty would be in attendance and available to receive late enrollments. He pointed out that enrollment as much as two weeks late could be accepted in hardship cases. This too was said with a straight face.

Finally one person did enroll. A waiter named T. M. Roberts enrolled during the extended enrollment period. At the semester's end, Roberts had a straight A record in all his classes. It may have been the extremely favorable student-teacher ratio (one to three) that explained his great success there. Then, again, maybe it was just because he set the curve on every exam in every class.

An immediate and more positive result of the *Sipuel* decision came not in Oklahoma but in Arkansas. After publication of the *Sipuel* decision, Lewis W. Jones, president of the University of Arkansas, announced that African Americans would be admitted to the university. Without litigation, the

University of Arkansas became the first public, all-white university in the south to admit an African American, Silas Hunt. Other blacks quickly followed. It was a pleasant coincidence that Silas and I had been classmates during my freshman year at Arkansas A & M, in Pine Bluff.

In Oklahoma, the state finally got around to paving the streets at Langston University. The lack of paving was one reason listed for the school's nonaccreditation. I suppose that Oklahoma reckoned that if accreditation would improve the law school's chances, a little paving was a small price to pay for that. Formal accreditation finally came. Better late than never.

Meanwhile, there was an interesting turn of events at Langston's bargain-basement law school. It received an application from Walter M. Harrison, a white former newspaperman. Harrison, with tongue in cheek, said he was ready to start classes immediately. Dean Hemry set aside his application, announcing that Harrison could not be admitted until he signed a statement that he had "Negro blood." Harrison had made a point and said he would not pursue the matter in court.

At the University of Oklahoma, mass meetings and rallies were frequent, some pro and some con. One day after a group of students demonstrated in favor of my admission, a second group of students demonstrated opposing my entry. This one ended with the protestors presenting Dr. Cross a petition with 282 signatures asking that segregation be continued. For drama, it hardly matched the previous day's closing, when the first group had burned the Constitution and Bill of Rights. Finally, after two demonstrations within two days, President Cross ordered no more rallies without administrative permission.

Amid all the confusion and turmoil, Oklahoma's public officials contemplated the worst-case scenario: that other blacks would apply to the University of Oklahoma in other disciplines. Dunjee had stated on several occasions since the beginning of the *Sipuel* case that Oklahoma could not afford to set up separate graduate and professional schools (including medicine) to accommodate all black aspirants. The editor had not been bluffing. In the high-stakes poker game of separate but equal education, such was precisely the strategy foreseen in our original petition—the financial self-implosion of segregation. When the state had gone ahead anyway with the fictitious but expensive law school, Dunjee and others prepared to call and raise.

On January 28, 1948, six African Americans appeared at Dr. Cross's office to apply en masse to six different graduate programs at the University of Oklahoma. They were Mauderie Hancock Wilson, Moseal A. Dillon, Ivory Tatum, Helen Holmes, James Bond, and George McLaurin. The first five sought graduate-level training in social work, zoology, commercial education, education, and architectural engineering. The sixth, McLaurin, was a retired teacher at Langston who sought a Ph.D. in school administration. They were frank to say that the basis of their position was the decision in the *Sipuel* case. As they understood it, *Sipuel* meant the state had to end the programs for its white students, admit the applicants to its all-white university, or provide immediate equal facilities.

Dr. Cross called Lloyd Noble in Ardmore, president of the Board of Regents of the University of Oklahoma, for instructions. A meeting was called for 10:00 A.M. the following morning in the administration building. Dr. Cross also called the state regents for official certification as to whether graduate schools existed for African Americans in the disciplines requested. They did not. Later that day, the state regents met in emergency session and referred the new problem to Attorney General Williamson. Williamson indicated that there might be a legal question whether the recent Supreme Court decision applied to the new applicants. No one—not Dr. Cross, his university's regents, or the attorney general—knew what move to make next.

I did. On January 30, 1948, my attorneys filed petition for a writ of mandamus in the United States Supreme Court under the title *Fisher v. Hurst*. This time the defendants named were different from those in the original *Sipuel* case in 1946. The petition named justices of the Oklahoma Supreme Court, Judge Justin Hinshaw of the Cleveland County District Court, and members of the University of Oklahoma Board of Regents as defendants. The petition alleged that the order of the Oklahoma Supreme Court created confusion and uncertainty as to my rights. It also said that the state's actions left in doubt the obligation of state officials in providing equal protection. My attorneys did not specifically mention the Langston law school, but our position was that one student could never constitute a legitimate school of any sort.

This time we lost. By a divided vote, the Supreme Court refused our petition for mandamus. The majority's logic was narrow, so narrow that reality could not squeeze through it. They declared that the only question was whether or not the Oklahoma court of original jurisdiction (the district court of Cleveland County) had followed its original *Sipuel* mandate. In cold language, the Court brushed aside all of the shenanigans that Oklahoma had pulled since its original order to declare that "whether or not the order is followed or disobeyed should be determined by [the district court of Cleveland County]. The manner in which, or the method by which, Oklahoma may have satisfied, or could satisfy, the requirements of the mandate of the Court, is not before us."

The decision in *Fisher v. Hurst* meant that I had to start at the district level all over again. This time, I would have to prove what to me seemed perfectly obvious: that the school crowded overnight into a few spare rooms at the capitol—a school with precisely one student—was less than the equal to the well-established law school chosen by 552 (white) students in Norman. Amos Hall filed the necessary papers before the Cleveland County District Court in March 1948. Judge Hinshaw scheduled the hearing for May 24.

For this second district court appearance, Thurgood Marshall joined Hall at the trial level. Assisting both were two of the nation's most distinguished attorneys. They were

African Americans. Dr. James Nabritt was Charles Houston's successor as dean of Howard's law school. He was also a tireless advocate of civil rights whose earlier court victories had included the Supreme Court's 1938 invalidation of Oklahoma's discriminatory suffrage laws. Robert Ming was a professor of law at the University of Illinois and a veteran of similar cases at every level. Both Nabritt and Ming were also esteemed educators. Nabritt would eventually become Howard's president and also serve as a special delegate to the United Nations. Ming was a recognized authority on law libraries. Both were qualified experts as well as effective counselors. In addition, the team had assembled a distinguished army of witnesses, which included some of the nation's most prominent law deans and educators.

I could not have had better counsel or expert witnesses. Unfortunately, Oklahoma's laws and customs did not allow me to show the distinguished visitors much hospitality. On the first day of the hearing, court recessed two hours for lunch. Marshall, Nabritt, and Ming all stood, looking to Hall and me to identify Norman's best place for us to eat. We had to remind them that we were in an all-white town and no restaurant would serve any of us. Marshall solved our problem by collecting pennies and buying peanuts out of a vending machine there at the courthouse. There was a cold drink machine in the basement; thus we had lunch. Marshall jokingly said to me, "Ada, I'm going to try this damn lawsuit, and I'm putting you in charge of bologna sandwiches. Don't let this happen again." Happily I did not have to fulfill that duty. On the second day, a group of ladies in the community arranged lunch for us at a church. A downtown restaurant served us the last two days of the hearing.

Because no hotel in Norman accepted black guests at the time, Dunjee took care of housing our distinguished visitors in private homes in Oklahoma City. Marshall and Nabritt stayed with two sisters, Mrs. Mamie Goodman and Mrs. Myrtle Biglow Barnes. They had a lovely, spacious home on Northeast Seventh Street, in a nice, quiet neighborhood.

Both were excellent cooks, and they provided their guests lavish attention. The other attorneys experienced much the same in the home of Mr. and Mrs. Ernest Jones.

During the trial, my attorneys held strategy meetings each night in the Goodman-Barnes home. The four lawyers focused on what testimony they would try to get in the record the next day and what they would try to keep out. They also attempted to anticipate how Judge Hinshaw would rule on probable motions and objections. In fact, Marshall and Nabritt placed bets on the basis of their expectations. In the courtroom, Marshall usually sat on the right side of the table and Nabritt on the left. Legal pads, briefs, and assorted documents covered the entire tabletop. The papers also concealed ten or twelve quarters. During the course of proceedings, one side or the other would offer a motion. In each instance, as soon as His Honor ruled, papers started shuffling as quarters passed from loser to winner.

Bob Ming and I sat there with sly grins. Amos Hall considered this courtroom behavior a bit too risky. A very discreet and proper man, Hall usually sat with his chair pushed back from the table. He said that if the judge discovered what was going on he did not want to be involved.

On one occasion when the paper rattling was going on, the judge looked at our table in a perplexed and somewhat suspicious manner. Ming, Hall, and I were grinning and near laughter. The paper rattling ceased for the moment. Thereafter, Marshall and Nabritt were more circumspect, but they continued their friendly betting.

Marshall was a man of the law. He had great respect for justice, equality, fairness, and the United States Constitution. Why then this joking game in the courtroom while court was in session? I think it expressed his conviction that he was not going to get any justice in an Oklahoma court. On several occasions he told me that in our various hearings in Oklahoma courts we were merely making a record.

We commuted from Oklahoma City to Norman each day. Dunjee rode with Hall and I rode with Marshall, Ming, and

Nabritt. Marshall was the driver. Old Highway 77, a two-lane road, was fairly busy from eight to nine with morning work traffic. The drive could be made easily in forty-five minutes. We would leave shortly after eight to allow time for parking in downtown Norman. This schedule worked well the first day. The second day we ran into about a mile of construction that had begun earlier that morning. Traffic was detoured and reduced to a single lane. A flag man on each end controlled and alternated the north and south traffic. This congestion threw our schedule off considerably. No one talked as we inched along, each aware that we almost certainly would be late. Finally we were out of the congestion and increased our speed to the legal limit. We reached the courthouse a few minutes after the nine o'clock starting time and could not find a parking place nearby. We had to park almost a block away. We were late. The three attorneys and I literally ran the block, briefcases and books in hand, trying to cut down on late time. When we reached the courtroom Hall and Dunjee and both state attorneys were there, and the room was nearly filled with spectators. The bailiff notified the judge that we had arrived, and His Honor entered and called the proceedings to order. Judge Hinshaw made no comment about our tardy arrival until the end of the day. He then made the pointed announcement that the court would resume at nine o'clock the next day and all parties to the proceeding were expected to be in the courtroom at that hour.

Next morning we left fifteen minutes earlier and arrived in Norman with adequate time. About four blocks from the courthouse, however, the car slowed and began to jerk and jump. Slower and slower we went. Nabritt, sitting in the back seat, leaned forward and asked what was the problem.

Marshall shrugged. "I don't know. It looks like we're losing power," he said.

"Can't it go any faster? Pump the gas!" Nabritt demanded.

Marshall pumped his foot up and down—but I noticed from the front passenger seat that he was stamping the floor, not the gas pedal.

An upset Nabritt said, "Now, the man told us yesterday we had better not be late again, so if this is as fast as the car will go, pull over to the shoulder and let me out. I can run faster than this, and I intend to be in court on time."

Suddenly, Marshall roared with laughter, slapped the steering wheel, and solved the problem. He reached down and turned on the key that he had surreptitiously turned off to start our troubles—and his fun.

When required, however, Marshall could be no fun at all. He was practically vicious when it came to cross-examining the state's prize witnesses. He granted no respect at all to many of the state's so-called experts, including Oklahoma's chancellor of education. Marshall dismissed him as a two-bit politician, not an educator at all. If the man knew so much about schooling, and if he was so sure that Langston was the equal of any college, could he explain why its library was smaller than that at the McAlester state prison?

When Dean Hemry took the stand, Marshall tore him to pieces with such fury that it excited a little sympathy, even from me. One highlight came when Marshall read from the Langston law school's official bulletin about fees charged students to support publications edited at the school. He then asked Hemry if the school published a law journal—or anything else, for that matter. Dazed and confused, the dean said that he did not know. Marshall jumped all over that. "Well, you are the dean of the law school. Why are you charging these fees if you don't know about a publication? Is it not a fact," he hissed, "that you just copied verbatim the material contained in the Oklahoma Law School Bulletin?"

After a long while, Nabritt leaned across the table and told Marshall in a stage whisper, "Turn him loose, Thurgood." Sitting in the second row, Warren heard it clearly. Marshall waved his hand in a demeaning, dismissing way and sat down—not even paying the poor fellow the courtesy of excusing him from the stand.

When it came to our side's witnesses, Marshall aligned an impressive array of legal and academic authorities to testify

BACK IN THE OKLAHOMA
COURTS, THURGOOD
MARSHALL CONFERS WITH
HARVARD'S LAW SCHOOL
DEAN, ERWIN GRISWALD.

as expert witnesses. One, Dean Earl G. Harrison of the
University of Pennsylvania, testified that the Langston facility
could not properly be called a law school at all. Dr. Max Radin
of the University of California's Boalt Hall denounced the new
school as a farce. He said that a full student body was necessary because the exchange of ideas at the student level
brings out the best in students of the law. Dr. Charles Bunn,
chairman of the law curriculum committee at the University
of Wisconsin, testified that the student whose only exchange
is with a professor is at a severe disadvantage. He also said
that at the Langston school both the faculty and the student
body were too small to be effective. The dean of Harvard's
school of law, Erwin N. Griswold, and Walter Gellhorn, professor of law at Columbia, also labeled the Langston school
vastly inferior. Even a former dean of the Oklahoma law
school, John Hervey, testified that the schools were not
equal, as did Page Keeton, the current dean.

Easily our most impressive witness was a junior member of the university's law faculty, Henry H. Foster. Professor Foster took the stand, and Marshall asked his opening question about the Langston operation. Foster exploded. "It is a fake! It is a fraud! It is a deception!" he shouted.

So extreme and unexpected was Foster's outburst that Judge Hinshaw ordered a five-minute recess to allow the professor time to regain his composure. Afterward, Attorney General Williamson attempted to calm Foster with an innocent opening question on cross-examination.

"You have quite a bit of feeling in this matter, don't you?" Williamson asked.

Foster then exploded a second time. "Yes, I do! And about the cheap political chicanery of some people who are responsible for this disgraceful state of affairs!"

How do you answer that? What question can you ask? Well, Williamson next called Joseph McClure. Mr. McClure was an attorney who worked for a railroad. He thought that a school with a small student body (one!) could allow for a great deal of individual attention.

Judge Hinshaw took the case under advisement. He called us back to his courtroom on the morning of August 2 to announce his decision. Hall, Dunjee, Jimmy Stewart, Warren, and I went to the county courthouse to hear the judge pronounce that the Langston facility was substantially equal to the University of Oklahoma's law school. For that reason, he was denying our motion. He announced his decision with a straight face. I sat there and looked at him. I cannot say that I was shocked, nor even surprised. I was disgusted.

....

The public's reaction was mixed. The *Daily Oklahoman* printed three letters to the editor that it identified as being representative of the many it had received. Of particular interest was one that supposedly represented a moderate opinion. It spoke volumes about what was moderation at the time:

Ever since Ada Lois Sipuel Fisher has been making her fight to enter the University of Oklahoma I have doubted her desire for a higher education. Now that action has been taken I think it will convince any sensible individual that the only thing she cares about is to force her way into a school where Negroes have never gone.

If she were sincere about wanting to enter law school, why did she have to bring four Negro men with her when she made her appearance?

Mrs. Fisher would do well to pattern her life after Walter White, a Negro who could easily pass for a white man, but refuses to do so. He chose to remain a Negro and not try to force himself on white people.

You Negroes should read his article, "Why I Remain a Negro," in the January *Reader's Digest*.

EUNICE NOLEN, Oklahoma City

About the same time, the OU student newspaper ran what it apparently regarded as a sensible, evenhanded editorial on the matter. Under the title "Shall All This Be Sacrificed," the writer recounted all the good things African Americans enjoyed as citizens in Oklahoma during the 1940s. The editorial judged that all of these things had been accomplished by patience and goodwill. It cautioned that everyone must accept the decision of the court, meaning, I suppose, accept the fake law school. It closed with these words:

> [Now] in 1948 all the good that has been accomplished in all these years of patient effort is being threatened . . . by the intemperate course of extremists in both races. Extremists of both races are demanding that patience and forbearance and good will shall be exchanged for force and direct action. It is a golden opportunity for the agitators and troublemakers.

When I read those articles, I did not take the first one's suggestion. I did not need to resort to the scholarship of the *Reader's Digest* to know who Walter White was. White was the executive director of the NAACP, Thurgood Marshall's boss, and a central strategist behind years of civil rights struggles. The latest was my fight to "force [myself] on white people." It was he who had directed the "four Negro men" who had accompanied me to court.

Those men—and this woman—were neither "extremists," "agitators," nor "troublemakers." They were attorneys, and I wanted to become one. We all knew that the time for patience was past. We represented a race that had been in this country since 1619, before the Mayflower had dumped the Pilgrims on Plymouth Rock. Our patience and goodwill had earned us chains as slaves, scars as freedmen, and daily insults as second-class citizens.

Our men had fought for democracy in all of America's wars, but somehow they had not earned it for themselves. Our women could not use the restrooms for "White Ladies," only those marked "Colored Women," the latter dirty and smelly. Our children saw clean, glistening, water fountains in public places (including state and federal buildings) for "Whites Only"; but they drank from dirty, unkempt, and sometimes clogged fountains, whose water reeked of the bitter and permanent taste of racism. Nearly all of us had gone to public schools that were vastly underfunded, understaffed, and underequipped compared to white schools. Black teachers, among the best-educated people in our communities, received salaries roughly equal to white high school graduates but almost one-third less than that of white teachers of the same training, experience, and tenure. The same bigotry and inequality controlled employment, promotions, and salaries everywhere else.

Good things, Mr. Editor?

There were some good things, but nearly every one of them was the fruit not of patience and forbearance but of protracted and bitter legal action. Black citizens could serve on state juries—only because Charles Houston had persuaded the Supreme Court that the Constitution applied to Sapulpa, Oklahoma, too. In Oklahoma, African Americans could vote—only because James Nabritt had forced the Supreme

Court to invalidate the state's disfranchising laws. Black people were freed of the housing discrimination compelled by restrictive covenants—only because Thurgood Marshall had slain them before the high court. Municipalities could not arbitrarily draw lines to separate black from white neighborhoods—only because Roscoe Dunjee had refused to accept them.

So there I was. If I was an extremist, an agitator, a troublemaker, I was one right along with Walter White, Charles Houston, James Nabritt, Thurgood Marshall, and Roscoe Dunjee. I was in damned good company. And I was proud to be there.

That pride overcame any fears that I might have had. During the suit's early days, I noticed whispered voices cutting in on my phone calls to Oklahoma City. "That's her, she's the one," they said.

"Who's she talking to?"

"It must be that Dunjee fellow."

"Are you sure it's not that nigger lawyer?"

Later in the struggle, I had an uneasy experience on a public bus ride from Chickasha to Oklahoma City. The driver recognized me when I boarded. As an African American I sat on the one "colored" bench at the back. He watched me through the mirror about as much as he watched the road. He stopped at every store and filling station along the highway to tell people whom he was carrying on the bus. People would come outside and peer in the back windows. At one gas and beer facility, a red-faced, unkempt customer weaved out and boarded the bus so he could get a good look at that Negro girl who was causing all this trouble. When I told Dunjee about the incident, he advised me to avoid public buses. I could ride trains; otherwise, I traveled by private autos.

It was not fear but pride that directed me. It was also a thousand memories. One involved an earlier bus ride. In the spring of 1943 my Langston roommate, Velah C. Ross, invited me to go home with her to Pauls Valley. We went there with friends, but the two of us had to take the bus back to Langston. Pauls Valley had no bus station, only a bus stop in front of a restaurant on its main street. When the Greyhound bus arrived, we purchased tickets from the driver, boarded, and went to our places on the "colored" bench at the back of the vehicle. As whites began to board, they took up all of the front seats. The driver came aboard and told us to get off until all the whites had been seated. White passengers took all the white seats and then filled the "colored" bench also. The driver then let us back on, but we had to stand in the aisles until we reached Purcell and several whites got off. This cleared the back seat, and we could sit down. Teenage girls alone in a tense, hostile situation in a rural community, we were filled with humiliation, anger, and silent rage. It is now more than a half century later, but I know that neither my roommate nor I will ever forget that experience. One of the "good things" from the 1940s? I remember being one of those two youngsters in that hostile situation. Maybe that should have been my answer so many years later when the mayor of Detroit asked, "Why you?"

....

While my attorneys and I had been making the court rounds, the state had had to confront the problem posed by the six African Americans who had applied for six other graduate programs back in January of that year. Following the advice of Attorney General Williamson, who cited Okla-homa's continuing segregation requirements, the university had rejected all of the applicants. Everyone knew, however, that the Supreme Court's *Sipuel* decision made it merely a matter of time—and not much of it—before Oklahoma must face the same unpleasant alternatives my case had posed: close the programs provided to white students, admit African Americans at once, or create new sham programs somewhere else.

The first choice was unthinkable; too many mommies and daddies voted for the politicians ever to let that happen. It then got down to choices two or three, and that was where the NAACP's strategists wanted it. I was not going to let Oklahoma get away with a Jim Crow law school, and the others were not going to accept Jim Crow programs either. Moreover, taxpayers would not let Oklahoma throw up six more expensive Jim Crow schools, followed by a seventh, and an eighth, all the way down the line, one for every black applicant who might come forward. Oklahomans would have to recognize that they really had no choice at all.

In the spring of 1948 a committee of deans from the university and the agricultural college at Stillwater had reported that it would cost between ten and twelve million dollars just to construct at Langston the physical facilities to operate the six programs already requested. Even then, it would take four to five years to get the buildings on the ground. The deans calculated that annual operating costs would run around half a million dollars per year, and even that would not be enough to hire a faculty comparable to OU's. Add up all those numbers, divide the total by the estimated black enrollment in the new courses (twenty-five to thirty per year), and it appeared that Mr. Crow was becoming too expensive and troublesome to keep around much longer. In more formal, academic language, the deans unanimously recommended that Langston University be improved and strengthened.

The academicians' logic was no more effective in this instance than it would be in Judge Hinshaw's courtroom. Neither the governor, the attorney general, the legislature, nor the state regents did anything. Thurgood Marshall did. He returned to Oklahoma and selected one of the six to be the key plaintiff in a new legal struggle. His choice was George McLaurin.

In later years, Marshall said that "Mac" was academically qualified, he was willing, and because he was 54 years of age, his admission should not raise the old bugaboo of interracial marriages.

In July 1948 Marshall filed suit in McLaurin's name before a special three-judge panel of the federal district court for western Oklahoma. Judges A. P. Murrah, Edgar S. Vaught, and Bower Broadus accepted jurisdiction and handed down their decision on September 29. Keeping with *Sipuel*, it declared that the state must either admit McLaurin or discontinue its graduate program in education for white students. At the same time, the judges explicitly refused to strike down Oklahoma's segregation laws, saying only that "in this particular case they are inoperative."

By his reading of the opinion, Attorney General Williamson decided that the university would have to admit McLaurin, but he insisted that it would have to maintain segregation while doing so. Anyone who thought that possibility to be absurd (and I was one) could not have believed the outcome.

Accompanied by Marshall, Hall, and Dunjee, George McLaurin officially enrolled in four graduate education courses on October 13, 1948. At the time, the College of Education used several classrooms in the old Carnegie Building. All of McLaurin's classes were assigned to the same one: room 104. The scheduling was no accident. The large lecture room had a little anteroom (Marshall later termed it a "broom closet") off to its north side. Separated from the remainder of the room by columns, the anteroom allowed an occupant to peer out at a forty-five-degree angle to see the front of the room and the blackboard. Thus the choice.

It was under such surreal and humiliating conditions that George W. McLaurin became the first African American to attend the University of Oklahoma. By the end of the year about twenty others had also enrolled. All of them were completely segregated within the university. They had designated sitting areas in the classrooms and the library. They entered the cafeteria by a side door and sat at folding tables set up in a corner away from other diners, surrounded by a heavy iron chain, and manned by an armed guard.

McLaurin, a senior citizen when he entered, left the university at the end of his second semester because of unsatisfactory grades. His age and the humiliation he suffered probably affected his performance.

My case was tied up on appeal. Each time I applied I was referred to the Langston law school, until the sham law school ran out of funds and closed its doors on June 30, 1949—two weeks beyond the last day to enroll for the University of Oklahoma's summer session. Dr. Cross intervened and ordered the office of admissions to accept me on June 17. By that order Dr. Cross overstepped the state courts and boards of regents. I enrolled the next day, June 18.

It was already two weeks into the summer semester—precisely 1,251 days since the cold January day in 1946 when Mr. Dunjee, Dr. Bullock, and I parked illegally on the North Oval.

....

I had always expected that studying the law would be a rigorous and challenging experience. Entering two weeks late in an eight-week summer session added to the difficulty of being a first-year student. In that summer session, classes met every day, including Saturdays, and subject matter was covered rapidly. Every session was crucial for every student. But I was not just any student. I was "that colored girl"—the only "colored" person and the only female in the summer enrollment of more than three hundred white men. I drove myself that first day, parked in the distant student parking lot, and walked briskly to Monnet Hall—the "Law Barn," as it was known at that time. I was especially looking forward to one of my first two courses, the one on constitutional law.

The classroom for that course was very large and built on a step-up incline, with one row of seats on each of about six levels. In back of the last row of seats was a single large wooden chair behind a wooden rail. Attached to a pole on the back of the chair was a large printed sign that said COLORED. The room was about half-filled when I walked in. I did not look about, just walked straight ahead and up the levels to the chair.

Minutes later the door opened and in walked the instructor. I gasped. He was Maurice Merrill, the faculty member

FINALLY A LAW STUDENT,
ADA LOIS IS READY TO ENTER
MONNET HALL—THE "LAW BARN."

who had represented the state in opposing my admission before the Oklahoma courts and the United States Supreme Court. Now it was Professor Merrill who was going to lecture me on the meaning of the American Constitution.

Even on that first day, most of my fellow students made me feel right at home. After class Bob Blackstock and a group of students came to my chair and welcomed me. They said they were glad that the struggle was over and that I had finally been admitted. Several loaned me their notes covering the missed two weeks. Others tutored me to help me catch up. Afterward, I learned that I had no reason for apprehension concerning Dr. Merrill. In fact, he became one of my favorite instructors. Another was Henry H. Foster, who, I discovered, taught with the same enthusiasm with which he had testified.

All of that eased the situation, but it did not change it. For two and a half years of intense litigation, I had been the guinea pig, the slender, almost shy "colored" girl from a small rural community who dared challenge the power and resources of the sovereign state of Oklahoma. The litigation was finally over. As I sat alone in one of the enormous class-rooms of Monnet Hall, I realized I was still the guinea pig. After all the protracted legal battles and the vociferous public debate, would I make it as a law student?

In all the time that I was there, I never quite escaped a feeling of isolation. The faculty was always fair, and my fellow students were generally friendly. Still, I felt that I was being observed across campus and by much of the nation, watching to see if I succeeded as a student. Some persons honestly questioned the ability of blacks to cope and advance in a white academic arena. I was not yet a lawyer, but I felt that I already bore a strong burden of proof. I felt I must do well as the symbolic black student. In litigation I had enjoyed the support and constant counsel of Marshall, Hall, Nabritt, Ming, Dunjee, and others. Sitting in the large, unadorned rooms of Monnet Hall, I was alone. Law school is strenuous. It was more strenuous with the reality of aloneness. Some-times I would go into an empty classroom to study. When the rooms were empty, I always sat in one of the front seats. As time for class approached and other students arrived, I would gather my notes and books and climb the rows up to the "colored" seat.

I suppose my primary feeling during the three-year law school experience was the feeling of aloneness. Not lonely; I was usually too busy studying and commuting back and forth to be lonely. The feeling was aloneness. I was alone even though I was surrounded by more than five hundred fellow students. I had never attended school with whites, and most of them had not had much experience with African Americans, at least not on a level of equality.

....

In May 1987 my family and I attended the premiere of *Halls of Ivory* by James Vance. The stage play was presented at Stage I in Tulsa. It is the story of my two-and-a-half-year legal fight to batter down the segregation barriers at the University of Oklahoma, as well as the story of the experience of G. W.

McLaurin and other black students in the days immediately after the admission of blacks. The three-act play was shown in a darkened auditorium with spotlights on several separate stages. I'm glad the auditorium was dark. As I watched the recreation of those experiences I felt old hurts, angers, and feelings of frustration that I thought were long since dead. The darkness allowed me privacy.

African Americans have traditionally been subjected to prejudice and bigotry. We have been stereotyped as Aunt Jemima, Sapphire, Uncle Tom, and Sambo. We have sat at the back of buses and up front in curtained-off cubbyholes on trains. We have climbed stairs to the balcony in theaters. "Whites only" water fountains and restrooms were everywhere. We have cleaned, cooked, and entertained in clubs and restaurants in which we could not be served. We were relegated to lowest-level and lowest-paid jobs; last hired, first fired. We fought to defend our country and make the world safe for democracy in a segregated army. We traded in stores that in some places did not permit us to try on the dresses and hats we were purchasing.

I have tried to decide what racist action or situation over the years I have felt most acutely. There have been many, and all of them have hurt. Hate always hurts. I think perhaps walking past my classmates in the law school classroom and climbing the levels up to the "colored" chair was the most humiliating. I was finally there, enrolled as a student along with some one hundred other first-year law students. We all were young American citizens with at least a bachelor's degree. We all had met qualifications for admission, and we were there solely for the purpose of studying the law. I, however, was considered so different that I must sit apart from my peers. As I climbed the levels and rows of seats, I realized that all eyes were on me. What were they thinking? Was I walking erect and maintaining a calm demeanor? I must show no emotion. I had to be careful not to stumble. As I ascended the levels to my chair, I wondered why that particular experience was worse than others.

Maybe it was the aloneness, knowing the arrangement was directed toward one person: me. Would it have been less traumatic if several blacks were along with me? I doubt it. The basic reason for my despair was the fact that this discriminatory arrangement was not the act of one or a few "rednecks" or a few bigoted people. On the contrary, it represented the laws and public policy of the state. It was designed and implemented by the government of the state of Oklahoma. My state had resorted to this ridiculous scheme.

The paradox of the situation is glaring. Laws should represent the distilled essence of what is best in society. Yet in 1946 I was faced with a state statute that made it a misdemeanor for black citizens to attend classes with white citizens, with a penalty of one hundred dollars and five days in jail for each day of violation. Education should prepare persons to function in a democratic society. Schools and classrooms should create environments for the acculturation of persons of different ethnicity and backgrounds. The "colored" chair arrangement was not designed to accomplish that.

I had not realized the extremes to which the sovereign state of Oklahoma would go to protect Jim-Crowism until the United States Supreme Court handed down the *Sipuel* decision in January 1948. I was prepared for the prolonged battle through the courts. I anticipated attempts to delay and avoid a decision on the merits by resort to technicalities. Once the high court had decided that the out-of-state tuition plan did not meet the requirement of equal protection, I naïvely assumed that the state would obey the law of the land. I did not expect it would be happy, but I assumed it would be law abiding.

"Colored" chair notwithstanding, I was finally a student in the law school at the University of Oklahoma. I had fought hard to get there; I would now master the legal principles and statutes required for graduation.

I missed Warren so much during the prolonged litigation. I went to Rhode Island as often as I could arrange, but I wanted him here. I needed him more and more. He left the job in his brother's company and returned to Oklahoma early in 1948, to my great relief. He took a job in personnel at Tinker Air Force Base, just outside Oklahoma City. Nearly every morning of my matriculation at the law school, the alarm clock rang at 5:00 A.M. At seven, Warren and I were on our way, Highway 62 and then State Highway 9 to Norman, more than thirty-five miles. He would leave me in front of Monnet Hall and drive on to Tinker.

I would go to the coffee shop for coffee, usually alone, and return to class at nine. After two to three classroom hours, I had several hours of study time in the library and occasionally time to hang out with other students (mostly black, but a few white) from other disciplines and courses. At 4:30 I would be sitting on the steps of Monnet Hall, waiting to see the little Chevrolet turn in the North Oval.

"How was your day, honey?"

"Okay. How was yours?"

"Okay."

On my third or fourth day in a class in pleading and procedure, the instructor gave an exam. Each of us received a full page of facts, some relevant, some utterly irrelevant. The requirement was to draft a petition for our client, the plaintiff, who was suing for damages.

I had seen plenty of legal documents during my long ordeal, but I had no earthly idea how to draft one. I remember stating every trivial detail contained on the examination fact sheet, including the fact that the defendant was driving a blue Ford car, eating a large red apple, and wearing khaki pants and a polo shirt when he sideswiped the plaintiff's parked automobile. In a real-life situation, my client and I would have been dismissed instantly. As it was, it was the first and only exam I failed in law school.

The failure left me devastated. I held a brave face until I was alone in the car with Warren on our way home. Then I collapsed in tears. I felt certain that this one failure meant I would never make it in law school.

ADA LOIS CELEBRATING
GRADUATION WITH
WARREN FISHER

Warren put his arm around me as he drove and let me sob out my fears and frustration. Finally, he spoke. "Lois," he said gently, "you're giving this incident too much significance." He then assured me that I was an intelligent lady with a solid liberal arts education. He reminded me I had been in school less than a week. He said I had a good analytical mind and a loving, supportive family.

"Get your chin up. I love you and I know you can do it." Eventually, I returned his smile. That was my Warren.

I have always considered that Warren and I graduated together in August 1951. I was the one that wore the large black robe with purple velvet sleeve bands and the red and white hood, but Warren and I were both so proud. Together we had made it.

The week I graduated, Mr. Dunjee arranged a grand celebration. It was a highly publicized program at Calvary Baptist

Church in Oklahoma City. The four attorneys who had handled the case all flew in, and Thurgood Marshall made a wonderful speech. I received flowers and small gifts, including a surprise one from Assistant Attorney General Fred Hansen.

After the program, the people who had served in the long court battle enjoyed a private banquet at a local club. The owner closed the club to the public, while we dined and danced for a couple of hours.

....

In 1949, shortly after I began law school, Thurgood Marshall once again challenged Oklahoma on the issue of equality of treatment. At issue this time was the segregation of African American students within the university. Oklahoma had given him the perfect circumstances. George McLaurin heard the same lectures as his white classmates, but he heard them in a segregated seat. He read the same library books, but read them at a segregated study table. The same was true of all black students at the university. We ate at segregated tables placed apart in a corner with an iron chain around them and an armed guard attending. In every physical circumstance, African Americans received identical educational opportunities as their white classmates. Did the fact of our separation violate the Fourteenth Amendment?

On June 5, 1950, a unanimous United States Supreme Court answered yes. Those chairs, those ropes, those barriers—all amounted to Oklahoma's denial of constitutional rights to "equal protection of the laws."

The next day, I moved down to the front row. I have not sat in the back ever since. *McLaurin* made that possible. *Sipuel* made something else possible. If a state could not constitutionally ship adult students out of state for schooling because of race, if it could not set up fake schools for adult students because of race, if it could not constitutionally separate adult students because of race, how could a state do any of those things to children?

A lot of people were wondering that after 1950. Among them were the parents of Linda Brown, a little girl then attending a separate but equal school in Topeka, Kansas. It was this same Linda Brown in Kansas who gave Thurgood Marshall his next plaintiff. It was what all of us had done in Oklahoma that gave him his precedents. It was all of this that eventually gave one Mr. Jim Crow his long-deserved due.

THE STONE
....

When I first applied for admission to the University of Oklahoma in January 1946, there was an explosive reaction in Oklahoma and to some degree across the nation. Newspapers and radios shouted the news. In Oklahoma and the other sixteen southern states the notion was unthinkable. The very thought was preposterous. Some persons predicted violence.

Of significant import five years later was the fact that white newspapers and newscasts in Oklahoma did not carry the story of my graduation. Only the *Black Dispatch* in Oklahoma City and the *Tulsa Eagle* reported the news. Other black-owned newspapers and magazines across the nation announced the story. This was a case of no news being good news. In the period of five years, dozens of blacks had enrolled in OU and other traditionally white colleges without incident or fanfare. Within that narrow time frame, desegregation in higher education had become routine. It was no longer a news item. The people of Oklahoma had either accepted or surrendered to the principle of equal treatment in higher education.

During the long litigation, Warren and I were blessed to adopt a beautiful little girl. She was a curly-haired, dimpled little cherub in diapers. Right from the start, she was our own child, and that meant the child of both of us. Her adoption papers gave her the name Charlene Lois Fisher, but she was just as likely to call herself Charlene Warren Fisher. In fact, Lincoln School in Chickasha maintained her first records under the latter name.

There was never a doubt as to her identity and her central place in our family. During the long law school ordeal, every evening's romps with her gave Warren and me some of our few dependable and pleasurable diversions. She came to us as a lovely infant. Soon she became a happy, knock-kneed toddler. Two heavy braids of hair hung almost to her waist, and she had short, cropped bangs. Strangers often wanted to hold her and give her gum and candy. She glowed in the attention.

Warren enjoyed showing Charlene off as a toddler. There was a billboard in our community showing three monkeys: one with hands over eyes, another with hands over ears, the third with hands over mouth. Warren explained the message to his beautiful child many times: See no evil, hear no evil, speak no evil. She eventually would coach him, "Look, Daddy—see no evil, hear no evil, speak no evil."

Expecting to display her insight to visitors along for the ride one day, Warren pointed to the billboard and proudly said, "Charlene, tell us what the picture of the three monkeys means." Charlene looked and quickly answered, "They're picking fleas off each other."

Bruce Travis Fisher, our younger child, was born seven months after my graduation. He was born all-boy, beautiful, perfectly formed, and equipped with a lusty mealtime howl that kept all the other babies in the nursery awake. When he was an infant, he was macho even in his denim-covered plastic training pants. As a preschool toddler, he became known around the school ground as "Charlene's bad little brother." At age three he was shaving with a dull plastic scraper and tending the lawn with his toy mower.

Charlene somehow managed to get her share of the Sipuel smart mouth, and Bruce did also. He may have added his mother's acquired characteristics as a lawyer. Before he was in school, he decided to form a lawn-care company with some of his buddies, so he drafted articles of incorporation. All the boys pledged to:

1. Do a good job
2. No Fighting
3. No Play
4. Divide money equal

Bruce took the paper out and showed it to his business partners, and they set off to work. Within minutes he was back. Experience had already compelled him to make three amendments. They were so important that he was not as careful this time with his spelling. They were:

5. No Snatching
6. No Tatle Tale
7. No cusing

Together, Charlene and Bruce were typical older sister and kid brother—which is to say that they sometimes did not get along well. Big sister wanted younger brother to obey, but he had his own ideas. She could storm and threaten; he could throw rocks. I guess it was a standoff.

Sometimes, though, they were loving buddies who could hug and cuddle in a large chair in front of the television. They played a silly game called "big dog, little dog." Charlene would say, "Woof, woof," in a heavy, growling voice. Bruce would answer "Woof, woof," in a small, puppylike voice. The dialogue would repeat and repeat, growing louder with each round. It seemed to have no winning or losing points, and it would continue until their father or I could stand it no longer. "Shut up!" one or both of us would exclaim in frustration. They would then hug and laugh loudly, and the game was over. Other togetherness experiences were the occasions when their father insisted they improve themselves by watching a short opera or classical musical program on public television. Again they would cuddle in the big chair, this time to commiserate and pout together.

....

The first year and a half after my son's birth, I stayed home in Chickasha and enjoyed taking care of him. My legal practice was pretty much part-time with on old friend from my childhood days. Thomas McIlveen's family had been our neighbors on Dakota Street for more than twenty years. After attending an out-of-state law school (this was before *Sipuel*),

ADA LOIS OFFICIALLY
SIGNING THE
REGISTRY OF THE
OKLAHOMA BAR

he had returned home and opened a small practice. I joined
him during 1952 and 1953, taking just a handful of local cases.
These included a routine child-custody case (which I won)
and a damage suit (which I lost). None of the cases brought
much money. As a matter of fact, two of them were strictly
pro bono. I took them for the experience.

As it turned out, my most remarkable experience came
with the first pro bono case. The district court originally had
appointed McIlveen as attorney for the defendant—paying
him fifty dollars for his trouble—and he asked me to join in
the defense. Neither of us had defended a murder case
before. In court we discovered that the prosecution would
qualify the jury for the death penalty. It was a capital case,
with our client's life entirely in our hands.

The client was Viola Spencer. In the detailed and precise

language of the indictment, the state charged that on December 12, 1954, our client "willfully, unlawfully, feloniously, without authority of law, and with a premeditated design" had killed one Clarence Brown "by cutting and stabbing the person of the said Clarence Brown with a certain knife, then and there held in the hands of the said VIOLA SPENCER . . . thereby inflicting in and upon the body of the said Clarence Brown certain mortal wounds, from which said mortal wounds the said Clarence Brown did there languish and die." Left out of all of that language were some rather striking circumstances. One was that our client was black and her alleged victim white. Another was that the client was in her midseventies, the victim in his midtwenties. The last was that in the African American community the two were known to have been lovers.

The prosecutor refused to negotiate the case. There was plenty of evidence that Spencer had done the deed. Indeed, the state had no fewer than ten eyewitnesses to the crime. Also to be considered was the white community's strong opposition to interracial affairs, opposition that would not in the least be mitigated by the remarkable age gap in this instance.

During the prosecution's portion of the case, each witness testified to the facts at hand. The best I could do was to solicit admissions that they, the defendant, and the deceased all had been drinking liquor for better than an hour before the killing. The circumstances allowed me to hope that the jury would discount their credibility.

When it came the defense's turn, the only strategy I could come up with was a plea of self-defense. I tried to persuade the jury that my client lived in constant fear of Clarence Brown's recurring rages, which were usually self-induced by drink. I suggested that the old woman herself was somewhat senile and emotionally enslaved to her young lover. I showed them that he regularly spent the lady's old-age pension on liquor. He lived in her home but contributed almost nothing to living expenses.

My key witness was the client herself. I put her on the stand and had her testify that the deceased often had slapped her around and that she had every reason to be afraid of him. In addition she testified that he was intoxicated at the time of the killing. This also would be in her favor. I finished my direct examination feeling that I had done about as well as possible under the circumstances. Unfortunately, I swiftly learned that my inexperience had caused me to overlook one item. I had not prepared my witness for the cross-examination that followed.

Referring to the ten eyewitnesses, the prosecutor asked her what, if anything, they had said or done while she was busy cutting up the deceased. She blurted out angrily, "They didn't do nothing, and they didn't say nothing, because they knew if they did I would get them too."

I was so stunned I had to ask for a brief recess. Afterward, in my closing argument, I told the jury that although the old lady was legally sane, her outburst was evidence of her diminished mentality. The jury bought at least a portion of the argument and rejected the state's charge of first-degree murder. Instead my client received fifteen years for manslaughter. Under the circumstances, McIlveen and I felt we had won a victory for our client.

It may have been a legal victory, but it did not pay anything to speak of. Enough such victories and the Fisher family would face financial ruin. Thus it was that in 1954 we moved to Oklahoma City and I became associated with the African American partnership of Bruce and Rowan. I was not a partner, more an apprentice. The firm owned a very fine two-story brick building in a nice commercial neighborhood. I paid no rent but made up for it by doing much of the research. The firm had a good basic legal library, and I also used the law library at the county building. Bruce and Rowan steered small cases to me and assisted me in more complex cases that came directly to me. Mr. Rowan even accompanied me to hearings in Oklahoma City and other cities in the event I needed help.

Mr. Bruce was elderly and did not like to make long drives. Rowan could not drive at all. When either had a case in a distant county, I drove. I was introduced as co-counsel and thus was free to ask questions of witnesses. I was also included in private conferences in the court's chambers. In these situations I was given a token fee by the partners.

As a novice attorney I stayed fairly busy but was not making much money. Most cases were small ones, and the fees were correspondingly small. The largest fee I received was nine hundred dollars from a probate case. Perhaps more typical was a case in replevin for a milk cow wrongfully withheld from my client by a neighboring farmer. Such cases were held in justice of the peace courts, which were presided over by nonlawyers. Those courts have since been abolished. The justice of peace to hear our case was himself a farmer. We arrived at his place at the appointed time. His Honor was feeding his hogs, and we stood around and watched. Finally, the magistrate held court in his coveralls on his back porch. My client got his cow. I received another legal experience and a story to entertain the secretaries. I did not get much else, though.

Under the circumstances, Warren and I had to budget carefully to stay within his salary as personnel officer at Tinker Air Force Base. Our children were getting older and their requirements more expensive. One day in the summer of 1956 I ran into a friend, Wayne Chandler, in Randolph Drugstore in Oklahoma City. We had a fountain drink, and I told him that my practice of law was interesting but that I was becoming discouraged because I still was not making much money. Chandler told me that Langston University was in need of a high-profile person to handle its public relations. As he understood it, the job would be part-time and would allow me to continue my legal practice. I thanked him and said I would think it over.

Later that day I told Mr. Dunjee of the job and asked his advice. He picked up the phone and called Langston's president, Dr. G. Lamar Harrison. Dunjee told him that he had learned of the job opening and that I might be available. The president was delighted, and Dunjee set up a date for us to meet. We met, and I took the job.

The salary immediately improved the family finances. Beginning in August 1956 I went to Langston once or twice a week and occasionally visited high schools in various cities to talk with students. This left me an average of three days a week for my legal matters.

At the end of three years, the president called me to his office and asked if I would teach one class in political science and one in business law. If so, he would instantly double my salary. The Fisher family needed the money, and I soon discovered that I loved the teaching experience. Teaching and counseling students was better than visiting clients in jails and attending court beside a pigpen. Students were so eager to learn, so inquisitive and challenging. I became a full-time instructor.

Some persons asked me why I left the law and went to the university. My answer was (and is) because I wanted to. I was already in my thirties. I had finished college in 1945, and it was then 1956. For eleven years I had not made a living wage. It was time I began to do so. I loved working with bright-eyed, ambitious young people. If I ever decided to return to practice law, I could. I retained my membership in the Oklahoma bar. For the moment I knew that I could influence more young people in a classroom than I ever could in a courtroom. Besides, I knew that I had nothing to prove to anybody.

....

My return to the Langston campus gave me ample evidence of the changes that my case and other legal actions had encouraged. Well-paved campus drives covered the old red mud that I had detested as a student. Sidewalks finally connected with each other. They even led to and connected buildings. There were two three-story classroom buildings, a new science laboratory, and a substantially improved library.

In all these ways the school was finally almost equal to Oklahoma's other four-year colleges.

It was also considerably less separate. In time we began to attract white students. Eventually about one-third of the faculty (and more of the salaried staff) were white as well. Everyone could see the changes and improvements. The *Sipuel* case had forced the state to face its neglect of Langston University. There were also changes in the student body, which remained predominately African American. Compared to the students in my undergraduate days, they seemed much more mature and cosmopolitan. Television and other forms of mass communication accounted for part of the difference. Another explanation was probably their wider exposure to an America that for their parents had been concealed by the "whites only" signs.

Linda Brown's parents acted upon their readings of the *Sipuel* and *McLaurin* decisions. So had plaintiffs in cases in Delaware, Georgia, Virginia, and other places. In each instance they turned to the same tireless and fearless advocate: Thurgood Marshall. He found in my case and the others all the precedents that he would need in arguing and winning the cases collectively referred to as *Brown v. Board of Education of Topeka, Kansas* in 1954, when the United States Supreme Court ruled that there could be no such thing as separate but equal education. Admitting that separate education was inherently and inescapably unequal education, the Court finally placed a constitutional noose around Jim Crow's neck. The next year it sprang the gallows trap, holding in *Brown II* that the South must dismantle its dual school system "with all deliberate speed."

The South had maintained its separate but equal schools with a lot more separation than equality. It responded to the Court's order with much more deliberation than speed. Under the old shibboleths of "states' rights" and "nullification," the South greeted the order with a campaign of "massive resistance." Sometimes this meant evasions that matched the imagination of Oklahoma's creation of an instant law school and "colored" chairs—not to mention "colored" toilets, tables, and all the rest. In some places it meant ugly violence that attempted to replace the rule of law with the rule of mobs. What it never meant was any turning back. Desegregation came—painfully, begrudgingly, and slowly— but it did come.

In Oklahoma it came surprisingly quickly and relatively easily. While some other states postured and protested, Oklahoma quietly went about obeying the high court's orders in the 1950s. I like to think that one reason was that my state had already learned that compliance was acceptable and evasion impossible. If my case had taught Oklahomans nothing else, it would have been worth it in that regard alone.

Now at Langston as a professor, I was teaching the first generation of African Americans to begin college since the *Brown* decision. In teaching the history of the Fourteenth Amendment I always related the *Sipuel* story from the inside. I discovered that my students could not relate to the status of African Americans prior to 1946. When I spoke of Norman as an all-white town just as the university was an all-white school, a perplexed and surprised look shrouded their faces. When I talked of roped and chained sections for black people, I saw anger in their clenched lips and fingers. When I said my case was the beginning of the end of segregation, the class often applauded and whistled. During the remainder of the year I signed autographs.

My experiences served me as a counselor as well as a professor. As is sometimes true on college campuses, the president and his primary administrators were not well liked or trusted by a large number of the students. I was ready to agree that some of their suspicions and complaints were well founded. Knowing of my background and attitude about right and wrong, students often turned to me with their frustrations and problems. Sometimes I could talk them down and convince them that their complaints were common in all group living, that their problems in dormitories and other campus facilities were just part of that natural process. In

LANGSTON PROFESSOR
ADA LOIS FISHER

other instances my counsel was that the students should consider the consequences of any action they proposed. Every
action brought a reaction. My own life had taught me that.
Now I used that lesson with its corollary: if your planned
action is worth the risk, you must be prepared to deal with
the reaction. They knew of my experience, and my example
carried far more weight than words alone.

Along with all the physical improvements at Langston, it
still remained a human operation and subject to all the foibles
of human beings. These provided my greatest frustrations,
particularly with delays in repairs and in getting teaching
material and equipment. One very cold day in February there
was no heat on the second floor of Moore Hall, where social
science offices and classrooms are located. Teachers and students were forced to wear coats, scarves, and gloves in class.
I made repeated calls to maintenance asking for repairs. I

finally called the academic affairs office to say I would dismiss all classes until repairs were made.

That brought action. The maintenance supervisor came with a small thermometer and placed it on a bookcase to see if temperatures were as bad as I had reported. I was furious. This seemed ludicrous. As soon as he left, I raised a window placed the thermometer on an outside window ledge, and covered it with snow. About a half hour later, when I heard his knock on my door, I quickly retrieved it, wiped it off, and placed it back on the bookcase. The man checked it, looked surprised, and quickly left. Pretty soon the heat came on. Mrs. Ruth Swain, an assistant professor in the department, looked on and laughed. She asked what the thermometer read. I said I had no idea, but it was probably whatever the snow read that morning.

More troublesome were some higher administrators. When I first went to Langston, the dean of academic affairs was an elderly man who was as contentious as he was conscientious. In addition to his legitimate administrative responsibilities, the dean regarded himself as something of a policeman. He regularly walked the halls, crouched beside doors to monitor class sessions, and watched the parking lot. He carried a little pad and made notes of who arrived when and what time each faculty person left. The man believed in professors being in their offices every minute they were not in class or the bathroom. Community involvement and quiet time for research and study did not count.

I refused to be intimidated by his control signals. Two days a week my classes ended at 2:00 P.M. On those "short days" I would meet him in the parking lot or pass him on the sidewalk, wave to him, and drive away. The dean would scold such practices in faculty meetings, but he never once personally confronted me.

I served under ten administrations, counting presidents, acting presidents, and interim presidents. Each was somewhat different in philosophy of administration. To most of those administrators, however, leadership meant scolding, threatening, and otherwise intimidating the faculty. I always enjoyed the first faculty meeting of each term. There new faculty would hear the president for the first time. I was amused to see their fear and apprehension as he blustered and threatened. It was standard fare for one president to invite anyone who did not toe the line to "hit Highway 33 and get to stepping." Tenured faculty generally ignored the threats and concentrated on academics. Many had twenty and more years' tenure and knew how to set and achieve practical goals. They were experts in helping a president with a program and also in defeating the program and frustrating his efforts without direct confrontation.

With two exceptions the presidents had strong backgrounds and experience in higher education. They generally sought to attract competent, experienced persons to the faculty and staff. One of the two exceptions directed most of his personal interest to promoting football. During the first semester of his administration, freshmen classes were grossly oversized, and two of the classes had no assigned instructors at all two weeks into the semester. Meanwhile, each faculty and staff person received five season tickets with instructions to sell them or buy them. Few if any complied. Another president who was filled with bluffs and bluster regularly strolled about the campus picking up bits of paper and other litter. Both the faculty and students called him Idi Amin.

As a Langston faculty member no less than as a Langston student, I was known to be highly individualistic. If I could not conscientiously and professionally accept a project, I just quietly ignored it. I knew the rule: you go along to get along. The fact was, though, I never tried very hard to do either. Most of the time I tried to practice the counsel that I gave the students. I tried to anticipate and weigh the consequences of my responses to what I regarded as inappropriate, foolish, or just plain wrong.

Sometimes my old habit of smart-mouthing got the best of me. For some time one of the administrators and I maintained a relationship of friendly enemies. He liked issuing orders and ultimatums to directors, department chairs, and faculty members. I delighted in sidestepping or challenging his orders. When presiding at meetings he affected an exaggerated manner and accent as if to enhance his academic authority. He also kept an eye on the corner seat in which I always sat at faculty meetings. He and I carried on prolonged and barely polite battles of letters, rebuttals, reminders, and memos. I rather enjoyed the give-and-take. I think he did also.

During one severe January ice storm the dean scheduled a meeting for 9:00 A.M. on a day in which no classes met. The highways were iced over and travel was risky, but I knew I had to travel from Oklahoma City to Langston (about thirty-five miles) and attend his meeting that morning regardless of road conditions. I arrived twenty or thirty minutes late, hoping I could quietly enter a side door and avoid a scene. When I entered the foyer, however, he was waiting and watching. Immediately he rushed toward me. "Now, Fisher," he said, "I simply will not tolerate your late arrival for a scheduled meeting. I will give you a written reprimand with a copy to the president and another copy to the director of your division—" I had to think quickly of some way to get rid of him.

I tried to interrupt. "Wait a minute. I must tell you something."

He cut me short. "I will not accept any excuse."

That exhausted any patience I still had. "Just listen to me," I said. "Then you can go ahead and do whatever you think you ought to do. I left home this morning while it was still dark. For two hours I have struggled on icy highways, trying to get here to your dumb meeting. Twice I lost control on curves and almost slid down deep embankments. Well, I prayed, 'Dear Lord, please take care of me out here on this dangerous, perilous highway. I'm here simply because my supervisor is mean-spirited. If, however, it is my time to go, so be it. I'm ready. But if I die, would you please kill him immediately? It's his fault. Please just drop him in his tracks. Thank you.'"

The good doctor look startled and became quiet. I struggled to hold a straight face during my performance. He suffered a chill at midmorning and had to go home. He was friendly for several weeks thereafter. My sham had worked.

Such experiences and frustrations aside, I thoroughly enjoyed my years at Langston. As was common for instructors at many small colleges in the 1950s, I taught sixteen and even eighteen credit hours per semester. Not only did I teach six three-credit-hour classes, but they were four different preparations. When I was assigned a class in history the second year, I returned to the University of Oklahoma for evening classes and summer sessions and earned a graduate degree in history. I spent every spare hour preparing lessons. Each time I walked into my classroom I was thoroughly prepared. I read not only the textbook and those on the suggested reading list but many others listed in the bibliography of these books. The news got around among faculty and students that the new teacher knew her subject matter well.

It is said that the influence of a teacher is almost infinite. It is true that such influence goes on in many ways and for many years in the life of her students. One example of such a teacher-and-student relationship began during my fourth year at Langston. The student was Virginia Horne. I frequently returned reports and various written assignments to her as being unsatisfactory. She had potential and ability but seemed to be testing me to see what she could get away with. She didn't get away with very much. Strangely, rather than resentment and hostility, there evolved mutual respect and later a deep friendship. Thirty years later, she and her husband, retired colonel Albert R. Spaulding, own and direct a company listed among the twelve largest minority companies in the United States. This is the kind of situation that rewards teachers that are able to sometimes touch, inspire, and influence a student.

In the classroom my role was less to fill students' heads with raw facts than to compel them to think and consider. The campus unrest of the 1960s and 1970s made that an even more important mission. Many students moved to the social sciences seeking ways to affect society. Many of those students were labeled as radical. I did not equate radical with criminal. Nor did I perceive the students as advocating criminal conspiracy or illegal acts. They wanted change, and they were impatient to get it. I could relate to their impatience with injustice and need for change.

For about two years in the 1970s, one group of students published an "underground" newspaper, the *Grapevine*. The paper was a curious mixture of poetry, national and state highlights, and campus news and gossip. Any faculty, administrator, or staff person thought to be involved in a misadventure would surely read about the misbehavior in the next issue of the *Grapevine*. Nothing was too private, intimate, or vulgar to be told in graphic street language. Each month copies would anonymously appear under office doors and in stacks in halls. Copies of the *Grapevine* were also mailed to alumni throughout Oklahoma and to officers of the National Langston University Alumni Association in cities throughout the United States. When the administration posted monitors at the local post office to watch for bulk mailing, the papers would be mailed from Oklahoma City, Lawton, Tulsa, and other cities around the state. One feature of the paper was the naming of two faculty members. One honoree was Bitch of the Month, the other Bastard of the Month.

No one admitted being involved in this publication, but I believed some of my majors were involved in publishing the paper. I called three of the most likely suspects to my office and told them if I was ever named the Bitch of the Month they probably would not graduate.

"We're not involved, Prof," they said.

I told them that if they were not, they had better get involved for their own protection. They slapped their legs and laughed heartily and left. My name was never mentioned in the paper. It was an honor I never received and never missed.

I did not seek administrative duties, but I received them. Over time I moved up the ranks from instructor to full professor, chairperson of the social sciences, and finally assistant to the vice president of academic affairs. In the last position I was director of the Langston University Urban Center in Oklahoma City. Progressively, such steps took me further from the classroom, but they brought me closer to home and to my family.

....

Howard Huggins and my baby sister, Helen Marie, met in Chicago in 1941. Helen had finished a program of study at Iowa State in Ames and had accepted a job in Chicago. Howard had recently completed studies at Saints Literary College in Mississippi. I suppose they were a natural couple. Howard was bold, vocal, and extroverted; Helen was quiet, dainty, and beautiful. Their first bond was their religious faith. They are both members of the Church of God in Christ. Howard is a holiness minister; Helen, the daughter of a late holiness bishop. Married in 1948, they have six children.

Lemuel married Clara Kirk, a beautiful girl he met while attending Howard University, in Washington, D.C. They had no children. They returned to live and work in Oklahoma, where he died of a heart attack in 1961. We grieved, but my grief and suffering was not to be compared to Mother's. My mother's grief was deep and very painful. For a parent to bury a child is contrary to the human relationship of child and parent.

After Lemuel's death her health began to decline. Mother had serious health problems in her later years. On one occasion she was hospitalized for two weeks at Baptist Memorial Hospital in Oklahoma City. This was back in the early years of desegregation, when African Americans and whites could share rooms if neither patient objected. Initially Mother had a two-patient room to herself. One day when I went in she told me she had a roommate. That particular day the roommate was in X ray, and I did not see her. The next day when I went in, the roommate was under sedation and sound asleep. On the third day's visit, the roommate was awake. When I pushed the door open and walked in, the roommate looked surprised. I had on a suit, heels, and a purse, so I was obviously not a nurse.

"Hi, Mother," I said. "How you doing?"

"Hi, Baby. I'm doing well."

As was my custom, I hugged and kissed her. I then sat on the bed, combed her hair, touched up her nails, and rubbed her arms and back with lotion. After a visit of about an hour, I promised to check by the next morning on my way to work.

"Bye, Mother. I'll see you tomorrow."

"Bye, Baby."

After a few moments' silence, the roommate decided to offer her judgment. "Lady," she said, since she did not know my mother's name (or obviously much else about her either), "Lady, that sure is nice of you to take that colored girl and raise her like a daughter."

"What do you mean 'like a daughter'? She *is* my daughter."

Roommate thought that over, swallowed hard, and said, "You mean you had a colored man?"

"Uh-uh," Mother answered.

Roommate lay back on her pillows and was silent for several thoughtful minutes. Finally she spoke. "Well, I never did. Course, I've had some friends who did."

Mother turned away and laughed into the pillow. When she was able to tell me about it, we both got a good laugh. I asked why she had not just told the woman she was African American, and she gave me the perfect answer: it was none of her business.

Mother's health began to decline rapidly in 1968. We feared for her living alone in the home place in Chickasha, and I persuaded her to come and live with us in Oklahoma City. I had a spacious home, which would afford her her own room and bathroom. She also had a telephone and television and writing desk in her room. She was a part of all family activities: going shopping, to church, and even on vacations with us. She loved mixing with the grandchildren.

She also took on her familiar roles in church and neighborhood activities in her new hometown. Soon, everyone—Warren, her grandkids, all of our neighbors—called her by one name: "Big Mama." In time she developed cancer, which metastasized, but she never lost her zest for life and sense of humor. She stayed as active as ever until one day when she was walking down the hall and felt a popping sensation in her hip joint. The doctors had told us that such would be the sign that the cancer had invaded her hip joint and that it would signal the end was near.

For the last few weeks she was unable to walk or care for herself, but Mother maintained her cheerful personality. She asked us to take her to a nursing home so she would be no burden, but Warren and I refused even to consider it. I told her that she had bathed and taken care of me, that now it was my turn and I intended to take it. One of her doctors tried to persuade us that amputating her legs might prolong her life, but none of us would consider that either. Mother was seventy-eight years old. She had lived a good, rich, and long life. She was not going to leave it as a stump. She did not. She did not fear death. As I stood beside her bed that day in March 1971, she motioned me to bend over. She kissed me, smiled, and was gone.

Life went on. The Fisher family had suffered loss before and had endured it. It did so again. Warren and I saw to it that Charlene received a first-class education. Today she is the divorced mother of two sons. The oldest of our grandchildren is Charlene's son Jerome Von Eric Factory. As the first, he was the pride and joy of both sets of grandparents. In our opinion he was a perfect little angel, with some few exceptions. One of his imperfect moments was the night he found Warren's prescription cough syrup, drank it, and became energetic and excitable. When we flagged him down we smelled the medication on his breath. A quick check of the bottle confirmed our fear. The child was a menace to persons and property for about ten minutes before he crawled in my lap and went to sleep. Fortunately, the bottle was nearly empty when he found it. Today he is a tall, quiet, handsome young man in the military service.

Khaldan Jermaine Factory, Charlene's younger son, is our second grandchild. More extroverted than his older brother, Khaldan loved going fishing with his grandfather Warren. The minnows he used as bait were sometimes as large as his catch, but every little fish caught was brought home, cleaned, and eaten. A cute, short, chubby little boy, Kahldan grew to be a tall, muscular youth who played all sports when he was in high school. He is now a student at Langston.

Bruce married Sharon McCloud and earned his bachelor's degree at Langston University and his master's (in history) at Houston's Texas Southern University. He also studied history and anthropology during a summer semester at the University of Ghana, in Africa. While he was there, he told his African fellow students about his family, mentioning that he had a mother named Ada Lois. "Is she African? Is she African?" they asked excitedly. That is how Bruce came to learn that my name is common among West Africans and means "first daughter." He also learned to modify it in the African style to Adanma, which means "beautiful firstborn." That is the name he gave his child, Adanma Sipuel Fisher. If that thereby preserves something of the African portion of her African American heritage, the American portion finds its manifestation in a nickname like those that I knew in Chickasha. "Sippi-do" we all call her—except when she misbehaves and briefly assumes the name of "Sippi-don't."

Emake McCloud Fisher is Bruce and Sharon's son and the youngest grandchild. "Man" is a typical dirty-faced, rough-and-tumble boy. He loves playing ball with his daddy, petting the dog, and throwing rocks at just about everything. On one of their visits, Man raced through the door to show me a large bandage on his forehead. I was immediately afraid that he had fallen and injured himself. He had not. He had a common childhood ailment known as "pink eye." The bandage on his head was his idea of a proper cure.

One day some time ago, when Emake and Adanma were two and six respectively, I overheard them singing:

Driving down the highway,
Highway 54,
A man let out a big one
that blowed off the door.
The car began to shudder,
The motor fell apart.
All because of one man
And one supersonic fart.

I interrupted and suggested they sing some other song.

"Okay," they said. They moved effortlessly to other songs in their repertoire: "Old McDonald had a farm . . ."

Has old Mr. Martin finally had his revenge?

....

Warren and I made our home and raised our children to adulthood on Springlake Drive in northeastern Oklahoma City. It is a street of spacious yards and rambling, ranch-style houses. Our lawn was always the showplace of the neighborhood. One of Warren's hobbies was tending the lawn and shrubbery. In spring the lawn was a deep, rich green and perfectly manicured. The shrubbery was carefully sculptured. The flowerbeds in front were bricked in and covered with scattered pine cones and decorative bark enhancing the beauty of the periwinkles, verbenas, and other flowering plants.

Warren spent quite a deal of money as well as time on the use of fertilizers and insecticides. Every few years the lawn was de-thatched and new topsoil added. One spring Warren ordered a large load of sandy topsoil. He specified the amount in terms of cubic yards. I only remember it cost $180. A dump truck brought the soil, and Warren had the driver drive the truck back and forth across the seventy-by-forty-foot yard with its tail down so as to spread the soil as it unloaded.

When the unloading was finished, Warren stuck his head through the door and yelled, "Lois, bring the man a check for a hundred and eighty dollars."

ADA LOIS DRESSED FOR A FORMAL EVENING WITH WARREN FISHER

"No," the driver interrupted. "I won't accept a check. I must have cash. Company policy."

"Lois!" Warren shouted. "Forget the check and bring this guy a shovel. Mister," he went on, "I want you to get every damn grain of your sand off my grass, put it back in your truck, and leave my property immediately."

"Wait a minute! May I use your phone to call my office?"

Warren sat on the edge of the porch for a long, silent moment as if thinking the request over. Then slowly and hesitantly:

"Well, okay, but be quick."

Warren suspected that the refusal to accept the check was based on a psychological or racial stereotype. The company was a large, well-established one, and our home and two automobiles would tend to indicate that we would not issue bad checks. The driver was caught in between. The call was made, and the check was accepted. That was my Warren.

Every spring the city allows residents to place large discarded items on the curb for pickup. Warren put an old lawn mower, a couple of electric fans, a leaky tub, and several other items on the curb. The newspaper had published the pickup dates for each quadrant of the city. On the published date for the northeast quadrant, the truck did not arrive. The next day Warren called the trash collection department to inquire about the delay. He identified himself: Warren W. Fisher, 4009 Springlake Drive. He was told there would be no pickup for northeastern Oklahoma City. The northwest, southwest, and southeast had been served, but the department had run out of funds. The person said Warren would have to wait for the next pickup—six months later—and promised to be sure to pick up our street then. Warren was furious. Listening to his end of the conversation and seeing his expression, I knew he was angry and likely to erupt. I ran to him and tried to take the phone, but I was too late.

"Okay, whenever. You don't have to rush. Take your time because I'll have all this crap in the river by the weekend."

I reminded him that he had fully identified himself before threatening to break the law. He shrugged and walked away. He did not care. That was my Warren.

Some of my friends call me stingy. I am not really stingy, but I do have an unusual spending pattern. The reason is that I set a goal for an amount of money I want to save or earn for investment purposes within a given time span, and I hold spending to an absolute minimum until I get there. I usually reach the goal within my specified time frame.

Several years ago I had almost reached an admittedly arbitrary total of savings I had set for the year. Very soon we would be ready to add it to our long-term investment holdings. Warren's small runabout car then started giving him trouble. Several trips to the garage failed to resolve the problems. The car was about seven years old, and Warren decided to trade it in and buy a new Subaru wagon. We would have to withdraw three thousand dollars from savings to make up the down payment.

We went to the credit union and up to the teller's window. I wrote the check, but when I handed it to the cashier, I suddenly started crying. I was that unhappy at taking the money out of an investment savings account. The cashier was caught by surprise. I can only imagine what she must have thought was going on there in front of her. I was standing there crying, and Warren was standing there with me, looking disgusted and annoyed.

Not knowing what to think, the cashier asked me, "Lady, are you okay? Are you making this withdrawal voluntarily?"

I was sniffling and wiping tears so hard I could not answer. I think the cashier was about ready to call security for a possible hostage scenario. Warren ended that with the declaration (loud enough for most of the credit union to hear), "Damn right she is withdrawing it voluntarily. That is my money and she is my wife. Lois, you shut your damn mouth and give the woman the check."

I did. We got the money and left. That was my Warren also.

I suspect that people who knew me only in my public or professional life would never have understood or expected the kind of life that Warren and I had together. I have often thought, though, that not many men could have been married to Ada Lois Sipuel. I was very, very fortunate to have found the one who could. For a long time I have known that I would have been lost without Warren Fisher.

Sometimes that has been literally the case. I have a tendency to get lost. I do not know why. It is not that I am thinking about something else or have other things on my mind when this happens. On the contrary: I have nothing on my mind at all. It is as utterly empty as the gray screen of a television after late night sign-off, and I gravitate to the nearest person or large object.

One example came on a crisp fall day when Warren and I stopped at a fast-food place for chicken. I went in to make the purchase. A middle-aged blonde lady in front of me placed her order, and I placed mine. The orders arrived simultaneously, and we each paid the cashier. The lady went out the door and across a wide parking lot to her car. I followed almost in step with her. She opened the back door of a white station wagon and placed her package inside. As I reached around her to place mine there also, I heard a car horn blow sharply. I looked up and saw Warren's frowning face two cars away. I snapped to alertness, grabbed up my package, and ran to our car. The blonde lady was left standing there looking perplexed.

One Christmas season a few years back I went to a shopping mall without Warren. It was a cold clear day as I ventured out. I completed my shopping without incident. I had parked my car, a gray Oldsmobile. On my return I proceeded to a green Oldsmobile, opened the door, and got in. I was several minutes getting my packages placed carefully on the front seat beside me. As I fastened my seat belt and prepared to insert the key in the ignition I heard a muffled sound behind me. I looked in the rearview mirror, and there sat a very old woman crying. The old lady was silver haired and was frail looking.

"Lady, please don't scream," I told her. "I am not kidnapping or robbing you. I thought this was my car. I have one kind of like this one."

As I left, I told the lady to be sure and lock her doors so she would be safe and to have a Merry Christmas. With that I raced away, got in my car, and drove away. It was another time that I needed Warren.

Once Langston's vice president of academic affairs, Jean Bell Maning, and I attended a three-day conference at a large luxury hotel. After the first night's meeting we attempted to go to our respective rooms. Jean was as disoriented as I. We walked up and down hallways and from one wing to another for about forty-five minutes. Our feet and legs were very tired. Thankfully some soldiers came by. They told us we were on the wrong floor.

In 1980 Warren went to our family doctor, J. W. Sandford, for a general checkup. Warren felt fine except for what we thought was a sprained muscle in his back. Dr. Sandford gave him the regular exam and also arranged for a spinal scan at

Baptist Hospital. The results hit us like an earthquake: a large aneurysm about an inch below Warren's heart. J. W. was not only our doctor but also a good friend. Instead of telephoning the news to us or even summoning Warren to his office, he waited until his office closed for the day and came to our home. He said he was not as concerned about Warren's reaction as he was mine. He gave us the news quietly and explained the condition in language a layman could understand. He then quickly selected the surgeon and hospital for Warren to have the necessary surgery. He observed the surgery process and hurried to the family waiting room to reassure us. Warren had come through the surgery well, and his chance of complete recovery was good. J. W. talked with me every day during the twelve-day hospital stay, encouraging and reassuring the children and me that Warren's recovery was right on schedule. Finally Warren was home again and we were back to our routine. We had seven more years together.

....

On October 20, 1987, I had been at my office at the Langston University Urban Center in Oklahoma City less than an hour. Elizabeth Jones, the executive secretary, and I had discussed a report I was scheduled to take to the faculty senate on the main campus of Langston University in the afternoon. A quiet voice from someplace said very clearly, "Go home." I had just left home about nine o'clock, and it was only ten o'clock now. Again the voice spoke, telling me to go home immediately. I told Ms. Jones that I would be back shortly and went to my car.

The voice—which I now know was the Holy Spirit—kept urging me to go quickly, very quickly. I found myself exceeding the posted speed limits and rushing signal lights. Parking in the driveway, I ran through the garage and utility room to the kitchen door. Warren was in a squatting position in the garden, tending young plants. Just as I walked out, he leaned to his left as if reaching out but continued leaning until he fell on his side. I jumped the porch steps and ran quickly to him. Kneeling and looking in his face, I knew he was dying.

Fright, panic, hysteria—I nevertheless ran to the kitchen phone and asked the operator to please get help immediately. I ran back to Warren screaming and praying; he was not breathing. Mr. A. C. Todd, a neighbor, ran over and joined me in prayer. The rescue squad arrived quickly. Another neighbor, Mrs. Velma Barnes, then came running. The three of us sat at the picnic table praying. The medics beat Warren's chest heavily and hit him with such strong jolts of electricity that his body bounced about like a toy. Neighbors from as far as a block away ran to the yard and cried out to God for Warren and me. Most were on their knees. Warren's heart started briefly, but en route to the ambulance it stopped again. The resuscitation procedure was repeated.

Eventually he reached the emergency room of Presbyterian Hospital. The children; my sister, Helen; her husband, Elder Howard Huggins; Warren's cousin the Reverend C. D. Fisher; and I gathered in the family room nearby. C. D. is my pastor, and he and his wife, Vivian, are warm, lovely friends as well. Finally the chaplain called me into the hall and quietly told me Warren was still alive, but barely. He said Warren had suffered severe brain damage and was not expected to make it through the night. I returned to the family room with the grim news. We kept praying. It was several hours before Bruce, C. D., Charlene, and I were permitted to see him in the intensive care unit. His color was gray, his eyes were glazed and rotating rapidly, and he was on sophisticated life-support systems. We approached quietly and stood near him silently for a moment. Finally Bruce spoke. "Daddy." Then loudly and forcefully, "Daddy." His father's eyes focused in his direction. I knew then that there was some level of awareness. I moved forward and touched him. His skin was cold.

"Honey, I know you can't talk and you probably can't see us, but we're here. If you can hear me, blink your eyes."

He blinked.

"I love you. Do you love me?"

He blinked.

"Okay, you hang in there. We'll get through this together."

He blinked.

We returned and rejoined the family group in prayer.

Warren was in the intensive care unit for eight days, then moved to critical care for two weeks. By the time he was discharged he showed no sign of brain damage. The doctor said it was a miracle. Everyone said it was a miracle that he even lived. Three weeks after entering the hospital, he sat up in bed and prepared all the necessary insurance papers. After he was released, he prepared our joint income tax for 1987. One doctor said he had already regained 90 percent of his mental capacity and was still improving. I told him 90 percent was good enough because that was about all I had still working. The family was together again at home. My mind turned to Scripture, especially the Old Testament verse in which the prophet declares, "And it shall come to pass that before they even ask I will answer and while they are still calling I will hear" (Isaiah 65:24).

Warren died suddenly on December 5, 1987. A dark, heavy curtain falls. No light penetrates it, only deep darkness. It smothers and crushes you. Not even shadows, just darkness and shock. Numbness. Later would come hurt, the kind of hurt I had never felt. Pain so intense that it prohibits speech. The only sound is the silent screaming in your mind. Pain—mental and physical. No, no. How can your whole life so suddenly end? All your hopes and dreams instantly vanish and you are left crushed. O Lord, can I please go with him? What else is there? Day fades into night and then it is day— and night again.

People rush about. Phones and doorbells sound as at a great distance. Arms reach out to you. Friends cry with you. The house fills with people and flowers and food. Plans must quickly be made. Forms must be signed, decisions made. Thankfully, Bruce and Charlene took over to handle program and burial arrangements. After a week or so I had emerged from complete blackness into a heavy fog. I can now see—but not very far or very clearly. I want to join him. There is nothing left that really matters. You look forward to the end of each day and pray for a few hours of merciful sleep.

Grief is a complicated process. It cannot be avoided or even modified. You are eventually alone—you and grief, after forty-three years of reciprocated love. You must walk through grief; you cannot run. You feel shock, disbelief, rage, and unbelievable pain. You hate to go to bed at night because you cannot sleep. You hate to get up in the morning because you can only face another pain-filled day. Many tears later, you reach for your faith. It has to work—nothing else has.

The services at Followers of Christ ended. I do not even remember the trip to Chickasha, where the family plot is located. I am told the motorcade was quite long. Good hometown friends who had known Warren and me for most of our lives waited at the open grave. A gentle wind was blowing, and the sun was shining. A military rifle salute preceded the clear, crisp notes of taps and the presentation of the flag. Our hometown friends presented a short, beautiful ceremony. The Reverends C. D. Fisher and Howard Huggins prayed. I remember the touch and support of our friends. I do not remember the trip home.

I said good-bye and buried Warren that warm winter afternoon. I have done so many times since. I am glad the sun was shining that December day in 1987. After it was over, I wrote this letter:

> Pastor C. D. Fisher and
> Members of Followers of Christ:
>
> During this period of grief following the loss of my husband, your prayers, flowers, food, gifts, and visitations have helped sustain my children and me. Thank you for your love and assistance. The musicians and choir members performed excellently, and the pastor's conduct of services warmed our hearts. One precious sister in Christ [Blanch Washington] visited me in my home. She held my hands and prayed with

me. She then sang a little song—a beautiful song of God's love for his children. Amen.

For almost forty-three years Warren was my husband, my teacher, counselor, best friend, and yes, even my very best pal and buddy. A friend from Chickasha [Bennie Black] recently said he seemed at times almost a parent also.

I thank God for having loaned me one of his best and brightest jewels. I said good night to Warren on December 5th. I'll see him again in the morning.

I remain with you in thought and spirit. When the hurt has sufficiently healed I will rejoin you in person. Continue to pray for me and the children. I love you all.

ADA LOIS

I have dealt with death on a personal level four times. My father, my brother, and my mother were all very close and dear to me. The pain of their passing was great. Warren's death was different. It was devastating. At the deaths of Daddy, Brother, and Mother, Warren was there, his arms around me, comforting me with his presence and by his words. Despite all that my children and friends could do, I felt alone at Warren's death.

Eventually I found ways to fill the time, if not the void. At his death, Warren had been retired for seven years, after spending thirty-four years at Tinker Air Force Base, where he eventually served as the affirmative action officer. In November 1987, just weeks before his death, I retired from Langston University. After Warren's death, I took a position in the legal department of Automation Research Systems, a firm in Alexandria, Virginia. The firm was founded and is owned by two longtime friends, Albert and Virginia Spaulding. Al, Va, Warren, and I had many happy times together when he was in the military. Their firm is the twelfth largest minority-owned business in the United States.

....

Over the years, I have gathered a great number of honors. In fact, my den's walls are covered with various plaques, awards, and citations. One that I am especially proud of is a green road sign. It designates nine blocks of a major east-west street in my hometown of Chickasha as Ada Sipuel Avenue. The Chickasha chapter of the Lincoln Alumni Association and Adolph Brown, its president, initiated the project. It was sponsored and guided through the council by another Lincoln alumnus, James Darn, who is a member of the city council. The city also designated July 3, 1993, as Ada Sipuel Fisher Day. The events of the day were arranged and coordinated by the association. Chickasha has come a long way since my parents moved there, since Lemuel, Helen, and I were born there, and since Henry Argo was lynched there.

The University of Oklahoma has come a long way also. Since that very cold day when Mr. Dunjee, Dr. Bullock, and I drove on the campus and broke the law by parking illegally and trying to register for law school, thousands of African Americans have attended, graduated from, and excelled at the University of Oklahoma. They have also done that at every public college in every southern state. None of them have had to sit in "colored" chairs or eat at "colored" tables, and I am glad for that.

Outside of a few history or law classes, it is likely that not many of them know all of the things that had to happen for that to be so. Not many, even in Oklahoma, have heard of the *Sipuel* case. Perhaps through this book, they will learn something of *Sipuel*. If they do, I want it to be a lesson that includes more than a decision in a single lawsuit. I want that lesson to include some sense of how black folks lived under Jim Crow. I want to give them some awareness of the things that people both famous and obscure endured to end it. I want to leave them some perception of the way that family, community, faith, and conviction can come together to make history, even in the case of a skinny little girl born on the wrong side of the tracks in a little town like Chickasha, Oklahoma.

DEDICATION OF CHICKASHA'S ADA SIPUEL AVENUE.
ADA LOIS IS IN WHITE HAT AT CENTER. TO HER IMMEDIATE RIGHT
ARE SON BRUCE AND DAUGHTER CHARLENE.

No longer skinny nor little, Ada Lois Sipuel Fisher has come a long way herself. In May 1991 the University of Oklahoma for the third time awarded me a degree. This time, there was no resistance at all, only a large ceremony at which the school awarded me one of the first Honorary Doctor of Humane Letters degrees in its one-hundred-year history. I believed it especially appropriate that Dr. George Lynn Cross was another in that very select group to receive an honorary degree. In April 1992 Governor David Walters appointed me a member of the University of Oklahoma's governing board of regents. The official ceremony was held in front of the old "law barn," Monnet Hall. It was a simple ceremony, nothing at all like the convolutions that the state had employed earlier to keep me out of that building. After the ceremony I went into Monnet Hall and was surprised to discover that my old lecture hall had disappeared in a recent conversion. Of course, that meant there was no sign that there had ever been a "colored" chair, and its disappearance was something of a conversion as well. On that day I remembered a Bible verse my father had read to me, the verse that proclaims: "The stone which the builders rejected is become the head of the corner" (Mark 12:10).

The decades between the 1940s and the 1960s were volatile years of struggle and change. African Americans fought fiercely for equal rights and the end of discrimination. In a proximate sense, the civil rights movement of the 1950s and 1960s grew out of the earlier desegregation cases in that it fired the imagination of the masses of young people.

Prophets look to the future for what will happen. Historians are as prophets whose domain is the past. They tell us where we now are and—more important—the direction of our travel. It is as a historian looking back over almost fifty years that I more fully recognize and appreciate the positive elements of those turbulent years. African Americans took their struggle to the streets, the churches, the political arena, and the courts. We keep reaching toward that goal of democracy. "We" are the American people.

Recent events also have caused me to reflect over the many changes that my life has witnessed. Recently, we had a reunion of the Lincoln School alumni. Several hundred people attended, many middle aged, a few even elderly. For all of the maturity and dignity that age and experience had brought us, we still called out to each other with familiar names. We all greeted one alumnus: "Hey, Hammer! Hammerhead!" Now a respected educator, he acknowledged the old nickname with a friendly wave and smile. I was not the plaintiff, the student, the attorney, the professor, or the regent. I was "Sip," and I was glad to be.

Writing this book gave me occasion to look back over the sum of my life. As I was finishing it I had another such occasion. In January 1995 my doctors told me that I had cancer. Like the cancer that took my mother, it is inoperable and terminal. As with her, its invasion of my hip joint will signal the end. The doctors' January estimate was that it would happen in approximately eight months. Five months have now passed.

At this moment, only my family, my pastor, and a few close friends know of my condition. I remain fairly active, and medication and radiation minimize the discomfort. Until my physical deterioration manifests itself, I want to be treated as I always have been.

How do I treat myself? I find that I was much more troubled by the earlier deaths of my loved ones than I am with the certainty and nearness of my own. I tell the few who know about my illness that I will have accomplished everything I wanted in this life when I finished this book. Because of my strong religious upbringing, I look forward to life beyond death. Sunset in this life is sunrise in the next.

CHRONOLOGY

....

ca. 1877	My father, Travis B. Sipuel, is born near Columbus, Mississippi.
1892	My mother, Martha Bell Smith, is born near Belarie, Arkansas.
1896	The U.S. Supreme Court, in *Plessy v. Ferguson*, upholds Louisiana's right to maintaining "separate but equal" railway carriages, setting the precedent for comprehensive segregation laws in the South.
1897	Langston University is founded as Oklahoma's "separate but equal" agricultural and mechanical college for African Americans.
1908	My parents marry in Dermott, Arkansas.
1918	My parents move to Tulsa, Oklahoma.
MAY 31– JUNE 2, 1921	Racial violence erupts in Tulsa following the arrest of Dick Rowland, an African American, for assaulting a white woman, Sarah Page. My father is taken into custody by the state militia; my parents' house burns. Shortly after, my parents move to Chickasha, Oklahoma.
February 8, 1924	I am born in Chickasha, Oklahoma.
May 31, 1930	Henry Argo is accused of rape and jailed in Chickasha. He is lynched in the early hours of June 1.
1938	The U.S. Supreme Court's decision in favor of Lloyd Gaines, a black applicant to the University of Missouri's all-white law school, is a landmark in desegregation history. Gaines disappears mysteriously before entering the school.

March 3, 1944	Warren Fisher and I marry.
May 1945	I graduate from Langston University.
September 1945	At the Oklahoma state convention of the NAACP, Thurgood Marshall outlines his plan to challenge state segregation laws by finding a qualified black applicant for the University of Oklahoma law school. Shortly afterward, I volunteer to be that applicant.
January 14, 1946	I apply to the OU law school and am rejected on grounds of race. Roscoe Dunjee announces that a lawsuit will be filed.
March 1946	With Dunjee, I begin a series of personal appearances to rally public support for the *Sipuel* case.
April 6, 1946	My attorney, Amos T. Hall, files a writ of mandamus in Cleveland County District Court, thus initiating legal action.
July 9, 1946	The writ of mandamus is heard and denied by Cleveland County District Judge Ben Williams.
July 11, 1946	Judge Williams denies Hall's motion for retrial. Hall prepares an appeal to the Oklahoma Supreme Court.
September 25, 1946	My father dies.
March 4, 1947	Thurgood Marshall and Amos Hall argue the appeal before the state supreme court.
April 29, 1947	The state supreme court upholds the district court's decision.
Spring 1947	OU cancels its annual Religious Emphasis Week because of controversy over an invited speaker, an African American chaplain.
September 24, 1947	My attorneys, in *Sipuel v. Board of Regents of the University of Oklahoma,* successfully petition the U.S. Supreme Court for a writ of certiorari.

January 8, 1948	Hall and Marshall argue the appeal before the U.S. Supreme Court.
January 12, 1948	The U.S. Supreme Court reverses the Oklahoma Supreme Court's decision and remands the case to that court.
January 13, 1948	The *Daily Oklahoman* publishes a poll indicating the 82 percent of law students at OU support my admission there.
January 14, 1948	I return to Oklahoma from Rhode Island, where Warren has been working in his brother's company, and prepare to enter OU's law school for the session beginning January 29.
January 17, 1948	The state supreme court issues an order directing the state board of regents to either close the OU law school or provide a separate school for me and others similarly situated, in accordance with the state's segregation laws.
January 24, 1948	R. T. Stewart, the chairman of the state regents, announces the creation of the Langston University College of Law. I receive a telegram from Langston's president instructing me to register on January 26.
January 24, 1948	An emergency fund-raiser in Oklahoma City raises one thousand dollars to help defray legal expenses.
January 25, 1948	I receive news that Cleveland County district judge Justin Hinshaw has refused Hall's request that I be admitted to the OU law school.
January 26, 1948	I reapply at OU and am again rejected.
January 28, 1948	Six African Americans apply to six graduate programs at OU. All six are later rejected.
January 30, 1948	My attorneys unsuccessfully file a petition for a write of mandamus, *Fisher v. Hurst*, in the U.S. Supreme Court.

March 1948	Hall files a new suit in Cleveland County District Court asserting that the Langston law school is not equal to OU's.
May 24, 1948	Hall and Marshall begin arguing the new suit before Judge Hinshaw.
July 1948	Marshall files suit before a federal district judicial panel in the name of George McLaurin, one of the six African American applicants to OU graduate programs.
August 2, 1948	Hinshaw rules that the two law schools are substantially equal.
September 29, 1948	Federal district judges rule that the state must admit McLaurin or discontinue its graduate education program for whites, in accordance with *Sipuel.*
October 13, 1948	McLaurin enrolls in OU's College of Education, the first African American to attend the University of Oklahoma.
June 17, 1949	With the Langston law school soon to close down, OU president George L. Cross allows me to enroll for OU's summer session.
June 18, 1949	I enroll at OU, two weeks into the summer session.
June 30, 1949	The Langston law school, lacking funds, closes.
June 5, 1950	The U.S. Supreme Court rules in *McLaurin* that segregated seating within a classroom is in violation of the Fourteenth Amendment.
August 1951	I graduate from law school.
1952–53	I join Thomas McIlveen's law practice in Chickasha part-time.

1954	*Brown v. Board of Education of Topeka, Kansas* reverses *Plessy*'s "separate but equal" doctrine.
1954	I join the partnership of Bruce and Rowan in Oklahoma City.
1955	The U.S. Supreme Court, in *Brown II*, orders southern states to dismantle their segregated school systems "with all deliberate speed."
August 1956	I become public relations director at Langston University.
1959	I become a full-time instructor at Langston University.
1961	My brother, Lemuel, dies of a heart attack.
March 1971	My mother dies of cancer.
1980	Warren undergoes surgery for a heart aneurysm.
May 1987	*Halls of Ivory*, a play by James Vance based on my legal battles to enter law school, premieres in Tulsa.
November 1987	I retire from Langston University.
December 5, 1987	Warren dies following a heart attack in October.
May 1991	I receive an honorary doctorate from the University of Oklahoma.
April 1992	Governor David Walters appoints me a regent of the University of Oklahoma.
July 3, 1993	Ada Sipuel Fisher Day in Chickasha.

THE CONTRIBUTORS

Ada Lois Sipuel Fisher is a retired attorney and educator. She was Professor and Chair of Social Sciences at Langston University, held several administrative posts at the Langston University Urban Center in Oklahoma City, and was a Regent at the University of Oklahoma.

Danney Goble, Director of American Studies at the University Center at Tulsa, is a specialist on Oklahoma since territorial days.

Robert Henry, Judge, U.S. Court of Appeals for the Tenth Circuit, was formerly Dean of the Oklahoma City University School of Law and Attorney General for the State of Oklahoma.

INDEX